AAT

Qualifications and Credit Framework (QCF)
LEVEL 2 CERTIFICATE IN ACCOUNTING

(QCF)

QUESTION BANK

Basic Costing

2012 Edition

First edition 2010
Third edition June 2012

ISBN 9781 4453 9485 5 (previous ISBN 9780 7517 9758 9)

British Library Cataloguing-in-Publication Data
A catalogue record for this book is available from the British Library

Published by

BPP Learning Media Ltd
BPP House
Aldine Place
London W12 8AA

www.bpp.com/learningmedia

Printed in the United Kingdom

CONTENTS

Introduction   v

Question and Answer bank

A NOTE ABOUT COPYRIGHT

Dear Customer

What does the little © mean and why does it matter?

Your market-leading BPP books, course materials and e-learning materials do not write and update themselves. People write them: on their own behalf or as employees of an organisation that invests in this activity. Copyright law protects their livelihoods. It does so by creating rights over the use of the content.

Breach of copyright is a form of theft – as well as being a criminal offence in some jurisdictions, it as is potentially a serious breach of professional ethics.

With current technology, things might seem a bit hazy but, basically, without the express permission of BPP Learning Media:

- Photocopying our materials is a breach of copyright

- Scanning, ripcasting or conversion of our digital materials into different file formats, uploading them to facebook or emailing them to your friends is a breach of copyright

You can, of course, sell your books, in the form in which you have bought them – once you have finished with them. (Is this fair to your fellow students? We update for a reason.)

And what about outside the UK? BPP Learning Media strives to make our materials available at prices students can afford by local printing arrangements, pricing policies and partnerships which are clearly listed on our website. A tiny minority ignore this and indulge in criminal activity by illegally photocopying our material or supporting organisations that do. If they act illegally and unethically in one area, can you really trust them?

INTRODUCTION

This is BPP Learning Media's AAT Question Bank for Basic Costing. It is part of a suite of ground breaking resources produced by BPP Learning Media for the AAT's assessments under the qualification and credit framework.

Basic Costing is computer assessed. As well as being available in the traditional paper format, this Question Bank is available in an online environment containing tasks similar to those you will encounter in the AAT's testing environment. BPP Learning Media believe that the best way to practise for an online assessment is in an online environment. However, if you are unable to practise in the online environment you will find that all tasks in the paper Question Bank have been written in a style that is as close as possible to the style that you will be presented with in your online assessment.

This Question Bank has been written in conjunction with the BPP Text, and has been carefully designed to enable students to practise all of the learning outcomes and assessment criteria for the units that make up Basic Costing. It is fully up to date as at June 2012 and reflects both the AAT's unit guide and the practice assessments provided by the AAT.

This Question Bank contains these key features:

- tasks corresponding to each chapter of the Text. Some tasks are designed for learning purposes, others are of assessment standard

- the AAT's practice assessments and answers for Basic Costing and further BPP practice assessments

The emphasis in all tasks and assessments is on the practical application of the skills acquired.

VAT

You may find tasks throughout this Question Bank that need you to calculate or be aware of a rate of VAT. This is stated at 20% in these examples and questions.

Approaching the assessment

When you sit the assessment it is very important that you follow the on screen instructions. This means you need to carefully read the instructions, both on the introduction screens and during specific tasks.

When you access the assessment you should be presented with an introductory screen with information similar to that shown below (taken from the introductory screen from one of the AAT's practice assessments for Basic Costing).

This assessment is in TWO sections.
You must show competence in BOTH sections.
You should therefore attempt and aim to complete EVERY task in EACH section.
Each task is independent. You will not need to refer to your answers to previous tasks.
Read every task carefully to make sure you understand what is required.

Where the date is relevant, it is given in the task data.
Both minus signs and brackets can be used to indicate negative numbers UNLESS task instructions say otherwise.

You must use a full stop to indicate a decimal point.
For example, write 100.57 NOT 100,57 or 100 57

You may use a comma to indicate a number in the thousands, but you don't have to.
For example, 10000 and 10,000 are both OK.

Other indicators are not compatible with the computer-marked system.

Section 1   Complete all 12 tasks

Section 2   Complete all 14 tasks

The actual instructions will vary depending on the subject you are studying for. It is very important you read the instructions on the introductory screen and apply them in the assessment. You don't want to lose marks when you know the correct answer just because you have not entered it in the right format.

In general, the rules set out in the AAT practice assessments for the subject you are studying for will apply in the real assessment, but you should again read the information on this screen in the real assessment carefully just to make sure. This screen may also confirm the VAT rate used if applicable.

A full stop is needed to indicate a decimal point. We would recommend using minus signs to indicate negative numbers and leaving out the comma signs to indicate thousands, as this results in a lower number of key strokes and less margin for error when working under time pressure. Having said that, you can use whatever is easiest for you as long as you operate within the rules set out for your particular assessment.

You have to show competence in both sections of assessments and you should therefore complete all of the tasks. Don't leave questions unanswered.

In some assessments written or complex tasks may be human marked. In this case you are given a blank space or table to enter your answer into. You are told in the practice

BPP
LEARNING MEDIA

assessments which tasks these are (note: there may be none if all answers are marked by the computer).

If these involve calculations, it is a good idea to decide in advance how you are going to lay out your answers to such tasks by practising answering them on a word document, and certainly you should try all such tasks in this Question bank and in the AAT's environment using the practice assessments.

When asked to fill in tables, or gaps, never leave any blank even if you are unsure of the answer. Fill in your best estimate.

Note that for some assessments where there is a lot of scenario information or tables of data provided (eg tax tables), you may need to access these via 'pop-ups'. Instructions will be provided on how you can bring up the necessary data during the assessment.

Finally, take note of any task specific instructions once you are in the assessment. For example, you may be asked to enter a date in a certain format or to enter a number to a certain number of decimal places.

Remember you can practise the BPP questions in this Question bank in an online environment on our dedicated AAT Online page. On the same page is a link to the current AAT practice assessments as well.

If you have any comments about this book, please e-mail paulsutcliffe@bpp.com or write to Paul Sutcliffe, Senior Publishing Manager, BPP Learning Media Ltd, BPP House, Aldine Place, London W12 8AA.

Question bank

Basic Costing Question bank

Chapter 1

Task 1.1

Look at the definitions below and match them to the correct term, putting a tick in the relevant column of the table below.

Definition	Cash transaction	Credit transaction
Transactions whereby payment is immediate		
Transactions whereby payment is to be made at some future date		

Task 1.2

Look at the definitions below and match them to the correct term, putting a tick in the relevant column of the table below.

Definition	Assets	Liabilities
Amounts that the business owes		
Amounts that the business owns		

Task 1.3

Look at the definitions below and match them to the correct term, putting a tick in the relevant column of the table below.

Definition	Management accounting system	Financial accounting system
Recording transactions of the organisation in the ledgers to prepare financial statements		
Recording transactions of the organisation to provide useful information for management		

Task 1.4

Look at the definitions below and match them to the correct term, putting a tick in the relevant column of the table below.

Definition	Budgets	Cost centre	Variances
An area of the organisation for which costs are collected together for management accounting purposes			
Differences that arise when the actual results of the organisation differ from the budgeted results			
Plans of the organisation for the next year in terms of money and/or resources			

Task 1.5

For each of the following activities, indicate whether it comes under planning, decision-making or control. Put a tick in the correct box.

Activity	Planning	Decision-making	Control
Whether to expand the business			
Budgeting how many products to produce			
Regular comparison of actual activities to plans and budgets			
Reporting variances			
Management preparing strategic and operational plans			
Management deciding which suppliers to use			

Task 1.6

Businesses can be set up in a variety of different ways.

Match the description to the types of business by ticking the correct box.

Description	Sole trader	Partnership	Limited company
A group of individuals who trade together to make a profit			
A business where the owner trades in their own name			
The owners delegate the running of the business to managers			

Task 1.7

Businesses make capital or revenue transactions.

Indicate whether the following transactions are capital or revenue by ticking the correct box.

Transaction	Capital	Revenue
Purchase of a motor car for the managing director in a printing business		
Purchase of a motor car by a garage for resale		
Payment of wages		
Rent on a workshop		
Extension works on a workshop		
Office furniture for the managing director		

Task 1.8

Businesses fall into different types based on the different industries in which they operate.

Identify which industry sectors the following businesses come under, ticking the correct box.

Description	Manufacturing	Retail	Service
Accountants, lawyers and other businesses which don't manufacture or sell a physical product			
The business buys in raw materials for making goods			
The business buys in ready-made goods which it sells on			

Task 1.9

What is the purpose of accounting?

Select the correct answer from the alternatives listed by ticking the box.

Definition	
To make decisions based on the best available data	
To control resources	
To record and accurately classify the transactions of the business	
To find the money to fund the owner's lifestyle	

Task 1.10

The table below lists some of the characteristics of financial accounting and management accounting systems.

Indicate two characteristics for each system by putting a tick in the relevant column of the table below.

Characteristic	Financial accounting system	Management accounting system
It supports managers in their control activities		
In a company it enables the production of accounts in a format required by law		
It provides information to assist in management decision making		
It ensures that all transactions are correctly classified as relating to assets, liabilities, capital, income or expenses		

Chapter 2

Task 2.1

Lascaux Ltd makes mosaic tiles for kitchens and bathrooms.

Classify the following costs by element (materials, labour or overheads) by putting a tick in the relevant column of the table below.

Cost	Materials	Labour	Overheads
Glaze for the mosaic tiles			
Gas charges for heating the workshop			
Employees mixing the glazes for the tiles			
Clay used in making the tiles			

Task 2.2

Carcassone Ltd has a bistro and wine shop.

Classify the following costs by nature (direct or indirect) by putting a tick in the relevant column of the table below.

Cost	Direct	Indirect
Wine bought in from a wholesaler		
Business rates for the bistro		
Wages of waiters and waitresses		
Salary of shop manager		

Task 2.3

Lyon Ltd makes guitars.

Classify the following costs by function (production, administration, or selling and distribution) by putting a tick in the relevant column of the table below.

Cost	Production	Administration	Selling and Distribution
Purchase of strings for making guitars			
Advertising the instruments in the city tourist information shop			
Wages of the bookkeeper			
Salaries of craftsmen making the instruments			

Task 2.4

Lille Ltd makes bread, cakes and pies for restaurants and its own chain of shops.

Classify the following costs by element (materials, labour or overheads) by putting a tick in the relevant column of the table below.

Cost	Material	Labour	Overheads
Wages of pastry cooks			
Salesperson's salary for the year			
Confectioner's cream used to fill the pies			
Gas charges for the ovens			

Task 2.5

Read the descriptions of labour costs below and match them to the correct term by putting a tick in the correct box.

Description	Basic pay	Overtime	Bonus
Amount paid for ordinary hours of work			
Hours worked above the normal hours stated in the employment contract			
Additional income for working more efficiently			

Task 2.6

Look at the costs listed below and indicate their nature and whether they are direct or indirect by putting a tick in the correct box.

Description of cost	Direct materials	Direct labour	Direct expenses	Indirect materials	Indirect labour	Indirect expenses
Patent royalties on each item made						
Factory supervisor's wages						
Lubricant for machinery						
Leather used to make shoes						
Hairdresser in a hair salon						
Telephone rental for administration office						

Task 2.7

Some costs can be incurred for a specific cost centre and some may be incurred for a range of cost centres jointly.

Identify whether each of the following expenses is specific to a single cost centre or is joint, by ticking the relevant box.

Expense	Specific	Joint
Repair of machinery used by one production line only		
Rent of workshop housing three cost centres		
Business rates for the workshop housing three cost centres		
Stationery used by the administration and payroll departments		
Photocopier used by the managing director's personal assistant only		

Task 2.8

Businesses make capital or revenue transactions.

Indicate whether the following transactions are capital or revenue by ticking the correct box.

Transaction	Capital	Revenue
Installation of new machinery		
Breakdown repairs on a faulty machine		
Fees of bookkeeper		
Purchase of new car for salesperson		

Task 2.9

Trindle Sewing Machines makes sewing machines. The business has recently received invoices for the following expenses:

Workshop rent	£4,500
Warehouse rent	£2,500
Office building rent	£1,000
Safety testing of the assembly department	£400
Overhaul of the grinding machines	£750
Training for salesperson	£500

The workshop houses five departments, with the following approximate percentage of floor space:

Grinding	30%
Assembly	25%
Testing	15%
Security	10%
Canteen	20%

The warehouse holds the stores and despatch departments, and the stores use approximately 70% of this area.

The office building contains the sales department (one cost centre) and administration, each using equal amounts of space.

Calculate the expenses to be collected for each of the cost centres and insert them in the table below. Show your working in your answer.

Cost centre expense	Working	£
Grinding – rent		
Grinding – overhaul		
Total Grinding		
Assembly – rent		
Assembly – safety testing		
Total Assembly		
Testing – rent		
Despatch – rent		
Stores – rent		
Security – rent		
Sales – rent		
Sales – training		
Total Sales		
Canteen – rent		
Administration – rent		

Task 2.10

For a provider of car insurance, classify the following costs by element (materials, labour or overheads) by putting a tick in the relevant column of the table below.

Cost	Materials	Labour	Overheads
Telephone costs for call centre			
Rent on call centre building			
Printer paper used for cover notes sent to clients			
Salaries of client advisers			

Task 2.11

For a taxi firm, classify the following costs by nature (direct or indirect) by putting a tick in the relevant column of the table below.

Cost	Direct	Indirect
Rent of booking office		
Diesel for taxis		
Wages of taxi drivers		
Licence for firm from taxi regulator		

Test 2.12

For a supplier of sandwiches to petrol station forecourts, classify the following costs by function (production, administration, or selling and distribution) by putting a tick in the relevant column of the table below.

Cost	Production	Administration	Selling and Distribution
Wages of workers making sandwiches			
Fee for website maintenance			
Purchases of bread			
Fuel for despatch vehicle			

Chapter 3

Task 3.1

Berlin Ltd makes stationery.

Look at the costs below and classify them into variable, semi-variable, and fixed costs. Place a tick in the correct box.

Cost	Variable	Semi-variable	Fixed
Employee paid a basic wage plus commission			
Rent of the factory workshop			
Print ink used for letterheads and logos			

Task 3.2

Hamburg Ltd processes sausages and other meat products. It has a factory, warehouse and shop which sells the products.

Look at the costs below and match them to the correct cost centre or profit centre by placing a tick in the relevant box.

Cost	Production cost centre	Service cost centre	Profit centre
Selling and marketing the products in the retail shop			
Mixing, filling and packing the sausages			
Storage in freezers in the warehouse			

Task 3.3

Baden is an accountancy partnership with several offices. Recently the partners decided to set up cost centres to run the partnership better.

Look at the costs below and indicate which cost centre each would be collected under by placing a tick in the relevant box.

Cost	Audit	Tax	Personnel
Payroll software for paying salaries and wages			
Annual purchase of Finance Act updates for the tax advisors			
Subscription to an audit advice helpline			

Task 3.4

Look at the statements below and decide whether they are True or False by placing a tick in the correct box.

Cost	True	False
Many fixed costs are only fixed over a certain range of output		
Variable cost per unit falls as output rises		
Direct costs are generally variable		
Fixed cost per unit rises as output rises		

Task 3.5

Look at the statements below and decide whether they are True or False by placing a tick in the correct box.

Cost	True	False
In a service organisation personnel would be a likely cost centre		
Selling and distribution would not be a cost centre in a manufacturing organisation		
Stores could be a cost centre in a manufacturing or a service organisation		

Task 3.6

Munich Limited makes outdoor gym equipment. It incurs fixed costs of £50,000 per year in relation to the manufacture of its outdoor treadmills.

Calculate the fixed cost per treadmill at each of the following four output levels and put your answers in the table below.

Output level of treadmills	Fixed cost per treadmill £
1,000	
10,000	
25,000	
100,000	

Task 3.7

Munich Ltd also incurs £35 per treadmill for variable costs in manufacturing the treadmills.

Calculate the total variable costs for the treadmills, completing the table below.

Output level of treadmills	Total variable cost £
1,000	
10,000	
25,000	
100,000	

Task 3.8

The managing director of Munich Ltd wants to know the total production costs for the treadmills.

Use the table below to fill in the figures which you have already calculated and also work out the cost per unit at each level of production.

Units	1,000 £	10,000 £	25,000 £	100,000 £
Costs				
Variable				
Fixed				
Total production cost				
Cost per unit				

Task 3.9

Complete the table below showing fixed costs, variable costs, total costs and unit cost at the different levels of production.

Units	Fixed costs £	Variable costs £	Total costs £	Unit cost £
1,000	37,200	19,800	57,000	57.00
2,000				
3,000				
4,000				

Task 3.10

A business's single product has the following variable costs per unit.

Materials	£4.50
Labour	£12.60

Total fixed costs are £75,000.

Complete the following total cost and unit cost table for a production level of 15,000 units.

Element	Total cost £	Unit cost £
Materials		
Labour		
Overheads		
Total		

Task 3.11

A business makes a single product. At a production level of 27,500 units the business has the following cost details:

Materials	0.2 kilos are used per unit. Materials cost £25 per kilo.
Labour	7,000 hours at £10.50 an hour
Fixed overheads	£35,000

Complete the table below to show the total cost at the production level of 27,500 units.

Element	Cost £
Materials	
Labour	
Overheads	
Total	

Chapter 4

Task 4.1

Patties Pastries is a bakery and cake shop.

Classify the following items as raw materials, work in progress or finished goods. Tick the correct box.

Cost	Raw materials	Work in progress	Finished goods
Christmas cakes left to mature			
Yeast for breads			
Simnel cakes in the cake shop			

Task 4.2

Patties Pastries wants to calculate the value of its inventory and has been told there are three methods it could use. The table below describes the three methods.

Put a tick against the correct method for each description.

Description	FIFO	LIFO	AVCO
Will give the highest inventory value if costs are rising			
Is the best method if inventories are combined, for instance cake mixes			
Uses the cost of the most recent inventories when costing issues			

Task 4.3

Patties Pastries has issued 100 cake boxes from its stores to the cake shop. Calculate the balance left under the LIFO method using the data below.

DATE	RECEIPTS		ISSUES	
	Units	Cost	Units	Cost
April 10	60	£120		
April 11	45	£135		
April 12	25	£75		
April 19			100	
April 27	70	£210		

Complete the table below for the issue and closing inventory values.

Method	Cost of issue on 19 April £	Closing inventory at 30 April £
LIFO		

Task 4.4

Patties Pastries buys in ingredients for its cake mix and issues these to the bakery where the cakes are made. In July it recorded the transactions below. Calculate the balance left under the AVCO method using the data below.

DATE	RECEIPTS		ISSUES	
	Tonnes	Cost	Tonnes	Cost
July 5	10	£30		
July 11	15	£45		
July 15	25	£100		
July 19			40	
July 28	30	£150		

Complete the table below for the issue and closing inventory values.

Method	Cost of issue on 19 July £	Closing inventory at 30 July £
AVCO		

Task 4.5

Complete an inventory record card for the transactions in the Task 4.4 using the pro forma below.

Inventory Record Card									
	Purchases			Issues			Balance		
Date	Quantity	Cost per tonne	Total cost	Quantity	Cost per tonne	Total cost	Quantity	Total cost	
		£	£	£	£	£	£	£	
Balance at 1 July									
5 July									
11 July									
15 July									
19 July									
28 July									

Test 4.6

A business has the following movements in a certain type of inventory into and out of its stores for the month of May:

DATE	RECEIPTS		ISSUES
	Units	Cost	Units
5 May	500	£1,200	
9 May	1,100	£2,750	
13 May			1,450
17 May	400	£1,100	
23 May	250	£700	

Complete the table below for the issue and closing inventory values.

Method	Cost of Issue on 13 May £	Closing Inventory at 31 May £
FIFO		
LIFO		
AVCO		

Task 4.7

Reorder the following headings and costs into a manufacturing account format on the right side of the table below for the year ended 31 December.

Heading	£	Heading	£
Manufacturing overheads	127,200		
Purchases of raw materials	120,000		
COST OF GOODS MANUFACTURED	570,700		
Closing inventory of raw materials	24,000		
Direct Labour	232,800		
COST OF GOODS SOLD	582,700		
Closing inventory of work in progress	24,000		
Direct expenses	102,700		
MANUFACTURING COST	575,500		
Opening inventory of work in progress	19,200		
Opening inventory of raw materials	16,800		
Opening inventory of finished goods	72,000		
DIRECT MATERIALS USED	112,800		
Closing inventory of finished goods	60,000		
PRIME COST	448,300		

Chapter 5

Task 5.1

Luanne runs a beauty salon and employs three assistants. They normally work a 35-hour week with a basic wage of £8.50 per hour. If they work overtime they are paid this at time-and-a-half.

Use the table below to complete the pay calculations for all three assistants for last week.

Assistant	Hours worked	Basic wage £	Overtime £	Gross wage £
Betty	35			
Hettie	38			
Lettie	41			

Task 5.2

Luanne has now decided to pay her assistants according only to the number of treatments they provide in a week.

The rate used is £15 per treatment successfully completed.

Calculate the gross wage for the week for the assistants in the table below.

Assistant	Treatments successfully completed in a week	Gross wage £
Betty	16	
Hettie	20	
Lettie	23	

Task 5.3

Luanne has decided to pay Lettie a bonus for her hard work.

Using the information in the previous task, calculate how much Lettie would earn if Luanne paid her an extra £1.50 per treatment for the treatments she completed where these exceed 20 in a week. Enter your answer in the table.

Assistant	Treatments done	Gross wage £	Bonus £	Gross wage + bonus £
Lettie	23			

Task 5.4

Luanne has been on a seminar where the speaker referred to the benefits of using piecework and time-rate payments. Luanne unfortunately forgot to take full notes and has asked you to fill in the gaps in her notes, which are in the form of a table.

Refer to the table and tick the correct column.

Payment method	Time- rate	Piecework
Quality is a priority as pay is the same no matter how much is produced		
This method gives employees an incentive to produce more		

Task 5.5

Luanne is wondering whether to adopt a signing-in system for her three hairdressers. At the seminar the speaker outlined the features of three types of signing-in system. Luanne is a bit confused as she can't remember which description refers to which system.

You can help her out by ticking the correct box in her notes.

Description	Attendance record	Signing-in book	Clock cards
Each assistant has a swipe card, which is used to register the time of commencing and finishing work			
A page for each assistant who signs the book when entering or leaving the building			
A calendar for each assistant that records their presence at work by a tick in a box			

Task 5.6

Luanne has adopted a clock card system for her three hairdressers. They are still paid at £8.50 per hour for a 35-hour week. Overtime is now paid at time-and-a-half for time worked in excess of seven hours on each weekday, and double time for any work done on a day at the weekend.

Calculate the gross pay of the hairdressers based on the clock card information summarised below and enter the details in the table.

	Hours worked		
	Betty	Lettie	Hettie
Monday	7	8	7.25
Tuesday	7	8	7
Wednesday	8.5	7.5	7
Thursday	7	8	7
Friday	7	7.5	7
Saturday	3		2

	Betty £	Lettie £	Hettie £
Total hours			
Basic pay			
Pay at time-and-a-half			
Pay at double time			
Total gross pay			

Task 5.7

A business pays a time-rate of £12 per hour to its direct labour for a standard 40-hour week. Any of the labour force working in excess of 40 hours is paid an overtime rate of time and a third per hour

Calculate the gross wage for the week for the two workers in the table below.

Worker	Hours Worked	Basic wage £	Overtime £	Gross wage £
B Calnan	40 hours			
N Imai	43 hours			

Task 5.8

A business uses a piecework method to pay labour in one of its workshops. The rate used is £2.30 per unit produced.

Calculate the gross wage for the week for the two workers in the table below.

Worker	Units produced in week	Gross wage £
L Akinola	187 units	
J Dunwoody	203 units	

Chapter 6

Task 6.1

Alexis runs a successful boat building business within Europe, which exports boats to Asia. His accountant recently recommended a coding system to help Alexis classify his costs and revenues. Each cost or revenue is classified in accordance with the table below. Thus a boat sale to Japan would be 9/200.

Use the table to code the transactions listed below.

Cost	Code 1		Code 2
Sales	9	European sales	100
		Asian sales	200
Production	8	Direct cost	100
		Indirect cost	200
Administration	7	Direct cost	100
		Indirect cost	200
Selling and Distribution	6	Direct cost	100
		Indirect cost	200

Code the following revenue and expense transactions for Alexis, which have been extracted from purchase invoices, sales invoices and payroll, using the table below.

Transaction	Code
Electricity charge for the upstairs offices	
Mobile call charges for sales reps	
Sales to Malaysia	
Sales to Italy	
Brass handles for boat decks	
Factory supervisor wages	

Task 6.2

Alexis would also like to analyse his costs according to materials, labour and overheads. He is looking at a coding system that classifies costs by their elements of cost (materials, labour or overheads) and then further classifies each element by nature (direct or indirect cost) as below. So, for example, the code for direct materials is M100.

Element of Cost	Code	Nature of Cost	Code
Materials	M	Direct	100
		Indirect	200
Labour	L	Direct	100
		Indirect	200
Overheads	O	Direct	100
		Indirect	200

Code the following costs, extracted from invoices and payroll, using the table below.

Cost	Code
Wages of boat builders	
Fees for bookkeeper	
Cost of buying timber	
Lubricants for lathes	
Business rates on Alexis' showroom	

Task 6.3

Alexis has now adopted a coding system and has been using it for some months now. He has asked you to update the code balances for July using the data below.

Code	Costs incurred in July £
010101	125.00
010102	3,000.40
010103	1,125.80
010202	433.20
010203	1,210.54
010301	44.00
010303	1,450.00

You will need to enter the costs incurred into the table below, which has the opening balances for July, and work out the closing balances at 31 July.

Code	Opening balance £	Update £	Closing balance 31 July £
010101	7,456.98		
010102	6,779.20		
010103	3,556.90		
010201	667.23		
010202	674.55		
010203	5,634.01		
010301	356.35		
010302	362.00		
010303	12,563.98		

Task 6.4

A manufacturer of porcelain and earthenware coffee cups uses a numerical coding structure based on one profit centre and three cost centres as outlined below. Each code has a sub-code so each transaction will be coded as **/**.

Profit/Cost Centre [Picklist]	Code	Sub-classification [Picklist]	Sub-code
Sales	01	Porcelain Sales	01
		Earthenware Sales	02
Production	02	Direct Cost	01
		Indirect Cost	02
Selling and Distribution	03	Direct Cost	01
		Indirect Cost	02
Administration	04	Direct Cost	01
		Indirect Cost	02

The codes have been used for a number of items in November. Identify from each code the profit or cost centre and the sub-classification to which it relates.

Code	Profit/Cost Centre	Sub-classification
04/01	▼	▼
02/02	▼	▼
03/01	▼	▼
01/02	▼	▼
04/02	▼	▼
01/01	▼	▼

Picklist:

Administration
Selling and Distribution
Sales
Production
Direct Cost
Indirect Cost
Earthenware Sales
Porcelain Sales

Chapter 7

Task 7.1

Siegfried Ltd has recently introduced a variance analysis reporting system. The managing director would like you calculate the variances suggested by the figures in the table, and let him know whether these are favourable or adverse.

Calculate the amount of the variance for each cost type and then determine whether it is adverse or favourable by typing F for favourable and A for adverse in the right-hand column of the table below.

Cost type	Budget £	Actual £	Variance £	Adverse/ Favourable
Direct materials	24,390	25,430		
Direct labour	11,270	12,380		
Production overheads	5,340	5,160		
Administration overheads	4,990	4,770		
Selling and Distribution overheads	2,040	2,460		

Task 7.2

It is now one month later and the managing director has asked you to analyse the variances summarised in the table below. You need to indicate whether they are significant or not significant using the dropdown boxes.

In Siegfried Ltd, any variance in excess of 5% of budget is deemed to be significant and should be reported to the relevant manager for review and appropriate action.

Examine the variances in the table below and select the correct option for the right-hand column.

Cost type	Budget £	Variance £	Adverse/ Favourable	Significant/ Not significant
Direct materials	23,780	360	Adverse	▼
Direct labour	10,460	660	Favourable	▼
Production overheads	5,330	318	Adverse	▼
Administration overheads	4,220	70	Favourable	▼
Selling and Distribution overheads	1,990	10	Adverse	▼

Picklist:

Significant

Not significant

Task 7.3

The managing director of Siegfried Ltd wants to know more about how budgets work. He has sent you a memo and asked you to confirm whether the statements he has made are correct.

Show if the following statements are True or False by putting a tick in the relevant column of the table below.

Statement	True ✓	False ✓
An adverse variance means actual costs are greater than budgeted costs		
A favourable variance means budgeted costs are greater than actual costs		

Task 7.4

It was noted from the performance report for Siegfried Ltd for last month that the following cost variances were significant:

- Direct labour cost
- Sales overheads

These variances need to be reported to the relevant managers for review and appropriate action, if required.

Using the picklist, select a relevant manager for each significant variance to whom the performance report should be sent.

Variance	Relevant manager
Direct Labour cost	▼
Sales overheads	▼

Picklist:

Production manager
Sales manager
HR manager
Administration manager

Task 7.5

A business has reported actual costs and variances as set out in the table below.

In each case, identify what the budgeted cost would have been.

Cost	Actual cost £	Variance £	Budgeted cost £
Production overheads	12,256	52 F	
Sales and distribution labour	8,407	109 A	
Administration consumables	4,751	236 A	

Answer bank

Answer bank

Basic Costing Answer bank

Chapter 1

Task 1.1

Definition	Cash transaction	Credit transaction
Transactions whereby payment is immediate	✓	
Transactions whereby payment is to be made at some future date		✓

Task 1.2

Definition	Assets	Liabilities
Amounts that the business owes		✓
Amounts that the business owns	✓	

Task 1.3

Definition	Management accounting system	Financial accounting system
Recording transactions of the organisation in the ledgers to prepare financial statements		✓
Recording transactions of the organisation to provide useful information for management	✓	

Task 1.4

Definition	Budgets	Cost centre	Variances
An area of the organisation for which costs are collected together for management accounting purposes		✓	
Differences that arise when the actual results of the organisation differ from the budgeted results			✓
Plans of the organisation for the next year in terms of money and/or resources	✓		

Task 1.5

Activity	Planning	Decision-making	Control
Whether to expand the business		✓	
Budgeting how many products to produce	✓		
Regular comparison of actual activities to plans and budgets			✓
Reporting variances			✓
Management preparing strategic and operational plans	✓		
Management deciding which suppliers to use		✓	

Task 1.6

Description	Sole trader	Partnership	Limited company
A group of individuals who trade together to make a profit		✓	
A business where the owner trades in their own name	✓		
The owners delegate the running of the business to managers			✓

Task 1.7

Transaction	Capital	Revenue
Purchase of a motor car for the managing director in a printing business	✓	
Purchase of a motor car by a garage for resale		✓
Payment of wages		✓
Rent on a workshop		✓
Extension works on a workshop	✓	
Office furniture for the managing director	✓	

Task 1.8

Description	Manufacturing	Retail	Service
Accountants, lawyers and other businesses which don't manufacture or sell a physical product			✓
The business buys in raw materials for making goods	✓		
The business buys in ready-made goods which it sells on		✓	

Task 1.9

Definition	✓
To make decisions based on the best available data	
To control resources	
To record and accurately classify the transactions of the business	✓
To find the money to fund the owner's lifestyle	

Task 1.10

Characteristic	Financial accounting system	Management accounting system
It supports managers in their control activities		✓
In a company it enables the production of accounts in a format required by law	✓	
It provides information to assist in management decision making		✓
It ensures that all transactions are correctly classified as relating to assets, liabilities, capital, income or expenses	✓	

Chapter 2

Task 2.1

Cost	Materials	Labour	Overheads
Glaze for the mosaic tiles	✓		
Gas charges for heating the workshop			✓
Employees mixing the glazes for the tiles		✓	
Clay used in making the tiles	✓		

Task 2.2

Cost	Direct	Indirect
Wine bought in from a wholesaler	✓	
Business rates for the bistro		✓
Wages of waiters and waitresses	✓	
Salary of shop manager		✓

Task 2.3

Cost	Production	Administration	Selling and Distribution
Purchase of strings for making guitars	✓		
Advertising the instruments in the city tourist information shop			✓
Wages of the bookkeeper		✓	
Salaries of craftsmen making the instruments	✓		

Task 2.4

Cost	Material	Labour	Overheads
Wages of pastry cooks		✓	
Salesperson's salary for the year			✓
Confectioner's cream used to fill the pies	✓		
Gas charges for the ovens			✓

Task 2.5

Description	Basic pay	Overtime	Bonus
Amount paid for ordinary hours of work	✓		
Hours worked above the normal hours stated in the employment contract		✓	
Additional income for working more efficiently			✓

Task 2.6

Description of cost	Direct materials	Direct labour	Direct expenses	Indirect materials	Indirect labour	Indirect expenses
Patent royalties on each item made			✓			
Factory supervisor's wages					✓	
Lubricant for machinery				✓		
Leather used to make shoes	✓					
Hairdresser in a hair salon		✓				
Telephone rental for administration office						✓

Task 2.7

Expense	Specific	Joint
Repair of machinery used by one production line only	✓	
Rent of workshop housing three cost centres		✓
Business rates for the workshop housing three cost centres		✓
Stationery used by the administration and payroll departments		✓
Photocopier used by the managing director's personal assistant only	✓	

Task 2.8

Transaction	Capital	Revenue
Installation of new machinery	✓	
Breakdown repairs on a faulty machine		✓
Fees of bookkeeper		✓
Purchase of new car for salesperson	✓	

Task 2.9

Cost centre expense	Working	£
Grinding – rent	£4,500 × 30%	1,350
Grinding – overhaul		750
Total Grinding		2,100
Assembly – rent	£4,500 × 25%	1,125
Assembly – safety testing		400
Total Assembly		1,525
Testing – rent	£4,500 × 15%	675
Despatch – rent	£2,500 × 30%	750
Stores – rent	£2,500 × 70%	1,750
Security – rent	£4,500 × 10%	450
Sales – rent	£1,000 × 50%	500
Sales – training		500
Total Sales		1,000
Canteen – rent	£4,500 × 20%	900
Administration – rent	£1,000 × 50%	500

Task 2.10

Cost	Materials	Labour	Overheads
Telephone costs for call centre			✓
Rent on call centre building			✓
Printer paper used for cover notes sent to clients	✓		
Salaries of client advisers		✓	

Task 2.11

Cost	Direct	Indirect
Rent of booking office		✓
Diesel for taxis	✓	
Wages of taxi drivers	✓	
Licence for firm from taxi regulator		✓

Test 2.12

Cost	Production	Administration	Selling and Distribution
Wages of workers making sandwiches	✓		
Fee for website maintenance		✓	
Purchases of bread	✓		
Fuel for despatch vehicle			✓

Chapter 3

Task 3.1

Cost	Variable	Semi-variable	Fixed
Employee paid a basic wage plus commission		✓	
Rent of the factory workshop			✓
Print ink used for letterheads and logos	✓		

Task 3.2

Cost	Production cost centre	Service cost centre	Profit centre
Selling and marketing the products in the retail shop			✓
Mixing, filling and packing the sausages	✓		
Storage in freezers in the warehouse		✓	

Task 3.3

Cost	Audit	Tax	Personnel
Payroll software for paying salaries and wages			✓
Annual purchase of Finance Act updates for the tax advisors		✓	
Subscription to an audit advice helpline	✓		

Task 3.4

Cost	True	False
Many fixed costs are only fixed over a certain range of output	✓	
Variable cost per unit falls as output rises		✓
Direct costs are generally variable	✓	
Fixed cost per unit rises as output rises		✓

Task 3.5

Cost	True	False
In a service organisation personnel would be a likely cost centre	✓	
Selling and distribution would not be a cost centre in a manufacturing organisation		✓
Stores could be a cost centre in a manufacturing or a service organisation	✓	

Task 3.6

Output level of treadmills	Fixed cost per treadmill £
1,000	50
10,000	5
25,000	2
100,000	0.50

Task 3.7

Number of treadmills	Total variable cost £
1,000	35,000
10,000	350,000
25,000	875,000
100,000	3,500,000

Task 3.8

Units	1,000 £	10,000 £	25,000 £	100,000 £
Costs				
Variable				
(units × (£35))	35,000	350,000	875,000	3,500,000
Fixed	50,000	50,000	50,000	50,000
Total production cost	85,000	400,000	925,000	3,550,000
Cost per unit	£85.00	£40.00	£37.00	£35.50

Task 3.9

Units	Fixed costs £	Variable costs £	Total costs £	Unit cost £
1,000	37,200	19,800	57,000	57.00
2,000	37,200	39,600	76,800	38.40
3,000	37,200	59,400	96,600	32.20
4,000	37,200	79,200	116,400	29.10

Task 3.10

Element	Total cost £	Unit cost £
Materials	67,500	4.50
Labour	189,000	12.60
Overheads	75,000	5.00
Total	331,500	22.10

Task 3.11

Element	Cost £
Materials	137,500
Labour	73,500
Overheads	35,000
Total	246,000

Chapter 4

Task 4.1

Cost	Raw materials	Work in progress	Finished goods
Christmas cakes left to mature		✓	
Yeast for breads	✓		
Simnel cakes in the cake shop			✓

Task 4.2

Description	FIFO	LIFO	AVCO
Will give the highest inventory value if costs are rising	✓		
Is the best method if inventories are combined, for instance cake mixes			✓
Uses the cost of the most recent inventories when costing issues		✓	

Task 4.3

The cost of the issue on 19 April under LIFO is £75 + £135 + (30 x £120/60) = £270.

Closing inventory at 30 April consists of 30 units at £120/60 = £60, plus the receipt of 70 units for £210.

Method	Cost of issue on 19 April £	Closing inventory at 30 April £
LIFO	270	270

Task 4.4

Method	Cost of issue on 19 July £	Closing inventory at 30 July £
AVCO	140	185

Task 4.5

Inventory Record Card								
	Purchases			Issues			Balance	
Date	Quantity	Cost per tonne	Total cost	Quantity	Cost per tonne	Total cost	Quantity	Total cost
		£	£	£	£	£	£	£
Balance at 1 July							0	0
5 July	10	3.00	30				10	30
11 July	15	3.00	45				25	75
15 July	25	4.00	100				50	175
19 July				40	3.50	140	10	35
28 July	30	5.00	150				40	185

Test 4.6

Method	Cost of issue on 13 May £	Closing inventory at 31 May £
FIFO	1,200 + (950 × 2,750/1,100) = **3,575**	700 + 1,100 + (150 × 2,750/1,100) = **2,175**
LIFO	2,750 + (350 × 1,200/500) = **3,590**	700 + 1,100 + (150 × 1,200/500) = **2,160**
AVCO	1,450/1,600 × (1,200 + 2,750) = **3,580**	700 + 1,100 + (150/1,600 × (1,200 + 2,750)) = **2,170**

Task 4.7

Heading	£	Heading	£
Manufacturing overheads	127,200	Opening Inventory of Raw Materials	16,800
Purchases of raw materials	120,000	Purchases of Raw Materials	120,000
COST OF GOODS MANUFACTURED	570,700	Closing Inventory of Raw Materials	(24,000)
Closing inventory of raw materials	24,000	DIRECT MATERIALS USED	112,800
Direct Labour	232,800	Direct Labour	232,800
COST OF GOODS SOLD	582,700	Direct Expenses	102,700
Closing inventory of work in progress	24,000	PRIME COST	448,300
Direct expenses	102,700	Manufacturing Overheads	127,200
MANUFACTURING COST	575,500	MANUFACTURING COST	575,500
Opening inventory of work in progress	19,200	Opening Inventory of Work in Progress	19,200
Opening inventory of raw materials	16,800	Closing Inventory of Work in Progress	(24,000)
Opening inventory of finished goods	72,000	COST OF GOODS MANUFACTURED	570,700
DIRECT MATERIALS USED	112,800	Opening Inventory of Finished Goods	72,000
Closing inventory of finished goods	60,000	Closing Inventory of Finished Goods	(60,000)
PRIME COST	448,300	COST OF GOODS SOLD	582,700

Chapter 5

Task 5.1

Assistant	Hours worked	Basic wage £	Overtime £	Gross wage £
Betty	35	297.50	0	297.50
Hettie	38	297.50	38.25	335.75
Lettie	41	297.50	76.50	374.00

Task 5.2

Assistant	Treatments successfully completed in a week	Gross wage £
Betty	16	240
Hettie	20	300
Lettie	23	345

Task 5.3

Assistant	Treatments done	Gross wage £	Bonus £	Gross wage + bonus £
Lettie	23	345	4.50	349.50

Task 5.4

Payment method	Time- rate	Piecework
Quality is a priority as pay is the same no matter how much is produced	✓	
This method gives employees an incentive to produce more		✓

Task 5.5

Description	Attendance record	Signing-in book	Clock cards
Each assistant has a swipe card, which is used to register the time of commencing and finishing work			✓
A page for each assistant who signs the book when entering or leaving the building		✓	
A calendar for each assistant that records their presence at work by a tick in a box	✓		

Task 5.6

	Betty £	Lettie £	Hettie £
Total hours	39.50	39.00	37.25
Basic pay (35 × £8.50)	297.50	297.50	297.50
Pay at time-and-a-half	1.5 × 8.50 × 1.5 = 19.12	4 × 8.50 × 1.5 = 51.00	0.25 × 8.50 × 1.5 = 3.19
Pay at double time	3 × 8.50 × 2 = 51.00	0	2 × 8.50 × 2 = 34.00
Total gross pay	367.62	348.50	334.69

Task 5.7

Worker	Hours worked	Basic wage £	Overtime £	Gross wage £
B Calnan	40 hours	480.00	0	480.00
N Imai	43 hours	480.00	48.00	528.00

Task 5.8

Worker	Units produced in week	Gross wage £
L Akinola	187 units	430.10
J Dunwoody	203 units	466.90

Chapter 6

Task 6.1

Transaction	Code
Electricity charge for the upstairs offices	7/200
Mobile call charges for sales reps	6/100
Sales to Malaysia	9/200
Sales to Italy	9/100
Brass handles for boat decks	8/100
Factory supervisor wages	8/200

Task 6.2

Cost	Code
Wages of boat builders	L100
Fees for bookkeeper	O200
Cost of buying timber	M100
Lubricants for lathes	M200
Business rates on Alexis' showroom	O200

Task 6.3

Code	Opening balance £	Update £	Closing balance 31 July £
010101	7,456.98	125.00	7,581.98
010102	6,779.20	3,000.40	9,779.60
010103	3,556.90	1,125.80	4,682.70
010201	667.23	0	667.23
010202	674.55	433.20	1,107.75
010203	5,634.01	1,210.54	6,844.55
010301	356.35	44.00	400.35
010302	362.00	0	362.00
010303	12,563.98	1,450.00	14,013.98

Task 6.4

Code	Profit/Cost Centre	Sub-classification
04/01	Administration	Direct cost
02/02	Production	Indirect cost
03/01	Selling and Distribution	Direct cost
01/02	Sales	Earthenware sales
04/02	Administration	Indirect cost
01/01	Sales	Porcelain sales

Chapter 7

Task 7.1

Cost type	Budget £	Actual £	Variance £	Adverse/Favourable
Direct materials	24,390	25,430	1,040	A
Direct labour	11,270	12,380	1,110	A
Production overheads	5,340	5,160	180	F
Administration overheads	4,990	4,770	220	F
Selling and Distribution overheads	2,040	2,460	420	A

Task 7.2

Cost type	Budget £	Variance £	Adverse/ Favourable	Significant/ Not significant
Direct materials	23,780	360	Adverse	Not significant
Direct labour	10,460	660	Favourable	Significant
Production overheads	5,330	318	Adverse	Significant
Administration overheads	4,220	70	Favourable	Not significant
Selling and Distribution overheads	1,990	10	Adverse	Not significant

Task 7.3

Statement	True	False
An adverse variance means actual costs are greater than budgeted costs	✓	
A favourable variance means budgeted costs are greater than actual costs	✓	

Task 7.4

Variance	Relevant manager
Direct Labour cost	Production manager, HR manager
Sales overheads	Sales manager

Task 7.5

Cost	Actual cost £	Variance £	Budgeted cost £
Production overheads	12,256	52 F	12,308
Sales and distribution labour	8,407	109 A	8,298
Administration consumables	4,751	236 A	4,515

AAT PRACTICE ASSESSMENT 1
BASIC COSTING

Time allowed: 2 hours

Basic Costing AAT practice assessment 1

Section 1

Task 1.1

The table below lists some of the characteristics of financial accounting and management accounting systems.

Indicate two characteristics for each system by putting a tick in the relevant column of the table below.

Characteristic	Financial Accounting	Management Accounting
It is based on past events		
Its purpose is to provide information for managers		
It is based on future events		
It complies with company law and accounting rules		

Task 1.2

Olsen Ltd is a manufacturer of garden furniture.

Classify the following costs by element (materials, labour or overhead) by putting a tick in the relevant column of the table below.

Cost	Materials	Labour	Overhead
Wood used in garden chairs			
Rent of factory			
Wages of carpenters in the cutting department			
Salary of the office manager			

Task 1.3

Curly Ltd is a hairdressing salon.

Classify the following costs by nature (direct or indirect) by putting a tick in the relevant column of the table below.

Cost	Direct	Indirect
Conditioner used on hair		
Insurance of salon		
Wages of salon cleaner		
Wages of hair stylists		

Task 1.4

Ascott Ltd is a manufacturer of children's toys.

Classify the following costs by function (production, administration, selling and distribution, or finance) by putting a tick in the relevant column of the table below.

Cost	Production	Administration	Selling and Distribution	Finance
Repairs to delivery vans				
Plastic used to make the toys				
Rent of the office building				
Bank interest				

Task 1.5

Fairway Ltd is a manufacturer of clothes.

Classify the following costs by their behaviour (fixed, variable, or semi-variable) by putting a tick in the relevant column of the table below.

Cost	Fixed	Variable	Semi-variable
Material used in the production process			
Advertising budget for the year			
Electricity costs that include a standing charge			
Labour costs paid on a piecework basis			

Task 1.6

Olsen Ld, a manufacturer of garden furniture, uses a numerical coding structure based on one profit centre and three cost centres as outlined below. Each code has a sub-code so each transaction will be coded as ***/***.

Profit/Cost Centre	Code	Sub-classification	Sub-code
Sales	100	UK Sales	100
		Overseas Sales	200
Production	200	Direct Cost	100
		Indirect Cost	200
Administration	300	Direct Cost	100
		Indirect Cost	200
Selling and Distribution	400	Direct Cost	100
		Indirect Cost	200

You are required to classify the revenue and expense transactions shown in the transaction column of the table below using the code column for your answer. The first two transactions have been coded for you.

Transaction	Code
Sales to Europe	100/200
Office staff wages	300/200
Office heating	
Warehouse rent	
Sales to Oxford, UK	
Sales to North America	
Materials to stain tables	
Factory canteen wages	

Task 1.7

Curly Ltd operates a hairdressing salon and uses a coding system for its elements of cost (materials, labour or overheads) and then further classifies each element by nature (direct or indirect cost) as outlined below.

Element of cost	Code	Nature of cost	Code
Materials	A	Direct	100
		Indirect	200
Labour	B	Direct	100
		Indirect	200
Overheads	C	Direct	100
		Indirect	200

You are required to classify the transactions listed in the transaction column of the table below using the code column for your answer. The first coding has been done for you.

Transaction	Code
Depreciation of equipment	C200
Salary of trainee hairdresser	
Wages of salon cleaner	
Cleaning materials used by cleaner	
Legal costs to renew lease of salon	
Colouring materials used on customers	

Task 1.8

Identify the type of cost behaviour (fixed, variable or semi-variable) described by each statement below by putting a tick in the relevant column of the table below.

Statement	Fixed	Variable	Semi-variable
Costs for 1,000 units are £2,000, made up of a fixed element of £500 and a variable element of £1,500			
Costs are £5 per unit at 500 units and £2 per unit at 1,250 units			
Costs for 750 units are £1,500 and costs for 1,250 units are £2,500			

Task 1.9

Classify the following costs as either fixed or variable by putting a tick in the relevant column of the table below.

Costs	Fixed	Variable
Direct materials		
Wages of production workers paid using a time-rate method		
Wages of production workers paid by a piecework method		
Rent for a factory used for production		

Task 1.10

Complete the table below showing fixed costs, variable costs, total costs and unit cost at the different levels of production. You are told that fixed costs are £12,000 and variable costs are £3 per unit.

Units	Fixed costs	Variable costs	Total costs	Unit cost
2,000	£	£	£	£
3,000	£	£	£	£
4,000	£	£	£	£

Task 1.11

Olsen Ltd is costing a single product, which has the following cost details:

Variable costs per unit

Materials	£2
Labour	£3
Total fixed costs	£80,000

Complete the following total cost and unit cost table for a production level of 20,000 units.

Element	Total cost	Unit cost
Materials	£	£
Labour	£	£
Overheads	£	£
Total	£	£

Task 1.12

Ironside Ltd makes a single product and for a production level of 24,000 units has the following cost details:

Materials	6,000 kilos at £20 per kilo
Labour	8,000 hours at £12 an hour
Overheads	£48,000

Complete the table below to show the unit cost at the production level of 24,000 units.

Element	Unit cost
Materials	£
Labour	£
Overheads	£
Total	£

Section 2

Task 2.1

Reorder the following costs into a manufacturing account format on the right side of the table below for the year ended 31 December.

Costs		Manufacturing account
Closing inventory of work in progress	£10,000	
Direct labour	£97,000	
Opening inventory of raw materials	£7,000	
Closing inventory of finished goods	£25,000	
Closing inventory of raw materials	£10,000	
Manufacturing overheads	£53,000	
COST OF GOODS SOLD	£200,000	
MANUFACTURING COST	£197,000	
Purchases of raw materials	£50,000	
Opening inventory of work in progress	£8,000	
Opening inventory of finished goods	£30,000	
PRIME COST	£144,000	
DIRECT MATERIALS USED	£47,000	
COST OF GOODS MANUFACTURED	£195,000	

Task 2.2

You are told the opening inventory of a single raw material in the stores is 600 units at £5 per unit. During the month a receipt of 400 units at £6 per unit is received and the following week 200 units are issued.

Identify the inventory valuation method described in the statements below.

Statement	FIFO	LIFO	AVCO
The issue of 200 units is costed at £1,200			
The closing inventory is valued at £4,320			
The issue of 200 units is costed at £1,000			

Task 2.3

Identify whether the following statements are True or False by putting a tick in the relevant column of the table below.

Characteristic	True	False
FIFO costs issues of inventory at the most recent purchase prices		
AVCO costs issues of inventory at the oldest purchase prices		
LIFO costs issues of inventory at the oldest purchase prices		
FIFO values closing inventory at the most recent purchase prices		
LIFO values closing inventory at the most recent purchase prices		
AVCO values closing inventory at the latest purchase prices		

Task 2.4

Olsen Ltd has the following movements in a certain type of inventory into and out of its stores for the month of March:

DATE	RECEIPTS		ISSUES	
	Units	Cost	Units	Cost
March 5	200	£600		
March 8	300	£1,200		
March 12	500	£2,500		
March 18			600	
March 25	400	£2,400		

Complete the table below for the issue and closing inventory values.

Method	Cost of issue on 18 March	Closing inventory at 31 March
FIFO	£	£
LIFO	£	£
AVCO	£	£

Task 2.5

Identify the following statements as True or False by putting a tick in the relevant column of the table below.

Characteristic	True	False
Direct labour costs can be identified with the goods being made or the service being provided		
Indirect costs vary directly with the level of activity		

Task 2.6

Identify the labour payment method by putting a tick in the relevant column of the table below.

Payment method	Time-rate	Piecework	Time-rate plus bonus
Labour is paid based on the production achieved			
Labour is paid extra if an agreed level of output is exceeded			
Labour is paid according to hours worked			

Task 2.7

Identify the labour payment method described by the following statements by putting a tick in the relevant column of the table below.

Statement	Time-rate	Piecework	Time-rate plus bonus
An employee is paid £432 for the 36 hours she has worked			
An employee is paid £400 for the 800 units she has produced			
An employee is paid £420 for the 35 hours that she worked and an extra £45 for efficient production			

Task 2.8

Greenside Ltd pays a time-rate of £10 per hour to its direct labour for a standard 35-hour week. Any of the labour force working in excess of 35 hours is paid an overtime rate of £15 per hour.

Calculate the basic wage, overtime and gross wage for the week for the two workers in the table below. Note: if no overtime is paid you should enter 0 for that worker.

Worker	Hours worked	Basic wage	Overtime	Gross wage
A. Singh	35 hours	£	£	£
S. Callaghan	40 hours	£	£	£

Task 2.9

Neilson Ltd uses a piecework method to pay labour in its factories. The rate used is 80p per unit produced.

Calculate the gross wage for the week for the two workers in the table below.

Worker	Units produced in week	Gross wage
G. Patel	300 units	£
A. Jones	400 units	£

Task 2.10

Ashton Ltd uses a time-rate method with bonus to pay its direct labour in its factory. The time-rate used is £12 per hour and a worker is expected to produce 5 units an hour, anything over this and the worker is paid a bonus of £1 per unit.

Calculate the basic wage, bonus and gross wage for the week for the three workers in the table below. Note: if no bonus is paid you should enter 0 for that worker.

Worker	Hours worked	Units produced	Basic wage	Bonus	Gross wage
A. Smith	35	150	£	£	£
J. O'Hara	35	175	£	£	£
M. Stizgt	35	210	£	£	£

Task 2.11

Identify the following statements as being True or False by putting a tick in the relevant column of the table below.

	True	False
A variance is the difference between budgeted and actual cost		
A favourable variance means budgeted costs are greater than actual costs		

Task 2.12

Greenside Ltd has produced a performance report detailing budgeted and actual cost for last month.

Calculate the amount of the variance for each cost type and then determine whether it is adverse or favourable by putting a tick in the relevant column of the table below.

Cost type	Budget £	Actual £	Variance	Adverse	Favourable
Direct materials	38,400	40,100	£		
Direct labour	74,200	73,000	£		
Production overheads	68,000	72,100	£		
Administration overheads	52,000	54,900	£		
Selling and distribution overheads	43,000	41,900	£		

Task 2.13

The following performance report for this month has been produced for Taplow Ltd as summarised in the table below. Any variance in excess of 8% of budget is deemed to be significant and should be reported to the relevant manager for review and appropriate action.

Examine the adverse (A) and favourable (F) variances in the table below and calculate the actual cost, indicating whether each variance is significant or not significant by putting a tick in the relevant column.

Cost type	Budget	Variance	Actual cost £	Significant	Not significant
Direct materials	£75,100	£6,000 (F)			
Direct labour	£64,500	£5,250 (A)			
Production overheads	£33,800	£2,600 (A)			
Administration overheads	£24,300	£1,900 (F)			
Selling and distribution overheads	£27,400	£2,250 (A)			

Task 2.14

It was noted from the performance report for Bourne Ltd for last month that the following cost variances were significant

- Direct materials
- Production overheads

These variances need to be reported to the relevant manager for review and action taken if required.

Identify, for the following significant cost variances, one relevant manager to whom the performance report should be sent.

Variance	Relevant manager
Direct materials	▼
Production overheads	▼

Picklist:

Administration manager
Distribution manager
Finance manager
Human resources manager
Production manager
Product development manager
Purchasing manager
Research manager
Sales manager
Transport manager

AAT PRACTICE ASSESSMENT 1
BASIC COSTING

ANSWERS

Basic Costing AAT practice assessment 1

Section 1

Task 1.1

Characteristic	Financial accounting	Management accounting
It is based on past events	✓	
Its purpose is to provide information for managers		✓
It is based on future events		✓
It complies with company law and accounting rules	✓	

Task 1.2

Cost	Materials	Labour	Overhead
Wood used in garden chairs	✓		
Rent of factory			✓
Wages of carpenters in the cutting department		✓	
Salary of the office manager			✓

Task 1.3

Cost	Direct	Indirect
Conditioner used on hair	✓	
Insurance of salon		✓
Wages of salon cleaner		✓
Wages of hair stylists	✓	

Task 1.4

Cost	Production	Administration	Selling and Distribution	Finance
Repairs to delivery vans			✓	
Plastic used to make the toys	✓			
Rent of the office building		✓		
Bank interest				✓

Task 1.5

Cost	Fixed	Variable	Semi-variable
Material used in the production process		✓	
Advertising budget for the year	✓		
Electricity costs that include a standing charge			✓
Labour costs paid on a piecework basis		✓	

Task 1.6

Transaction	Code
Sales to Europe	100/200
Office staff wages	300/200
Office heating	300/200
Warehouse rent	400/200
Sales to Oxford, UK	100/100
Sales to North America	100/200
Materials to stain tables	200/100
Factory canteen wages	200/200

Task 1.7

Transaction	Code
Depreciation of equipment	C200
Salary of trainee hairdresser	B100
Wages of salon cleaner	B200
Cleaning materials used by cleaner	A200
Legal costs to renew lease of salon	C200
Colouring materials used on customers	A100

Task 1.8

Statement	Fixed	Variable	Semi-variable
Costs for 1,000 units are £2,000, made up of a fixed element of £500 and a variable element of £1,500			✓
Costs are £5 per unit at 500 units and £2 per unit at 1,250 units	✓		
Costs for 750 units are £1,500 and costs for 1,250 units are £2,500		✓	

Task 1.9

Costs	Fixed	Variable
Direct materials		✓
Wages of production workers paid using a time-rate method	✓	
Wages of production workers paid by a piecework method		✓
Rent for a factory used for production	✓	

Task 1.10

Units	Fixed costs	Variable costs	Total costs	Unit cost
2,000	£12,000	£6,000	£18,000	£9.00
3,000	£12,000	£9,000	£21,000	£7.00
4,000	£12,000	£12,000	£24,000	£6.00

Task 1.11

Element	Total cost	Unit cost
Materials	£40,000	£2.00
Labour	£60,000	£3.00
Overheads	£80,000	£4.00
Total	£180,000	£9.00

Task 1.12

Element	Unit cost
Materials	£5.00
Labour	£4.00
Overheads	£2.00
Total	£11.00

Section 2

Task 2.1

Costs		Manufacturing account	
Closing inventory of work in progress	£10,000	Opening inventory of raw materials	£7,000
Direct labour	£97,000	Purchases of raw materials	£50,000
Opening inventory of raw materials	£7,000	Closing inventory of raw materials	£10,000
Closing inventory of finished goods	£25,000	DIRECT MATERIALS USED	£47,000
Closing inventory of raw materials	£10,000	Direct labour	£97,000
Manufacturing overheads	£53,000	PRIME COST	£144,000
COST OF GOODS SOLD	£200,000	Manufacturing overheads	£53,000
MANUFACTURING COST	£197,000	MANUFACTURING COST	£197,000
Purchases of raw materials	£50,000	Opening inventory of work in progress	£8,000
Opening inventory of work in progress	£8,000	Closing inventory of work in progress	£10,000
Opening inventory of finished goods	£30,000	COST OF GOODS MANUFACTURED	£195,000
PRIME COST	£144,000	Opening inventory of finished goods	£30,000
DIRECT MATERIALS USED	£47,000	Closing inventory of finished goods	£25,000
COST OF GOODS MANUFACTURED	£195,000	COST OF GOODS SOLD	£200,000

Task 2.2

Statement	FIFO	LIFO	AVCO
The issue of 200 units is costed at £1,200		✓	
The closing inventory is valued at £4,320			✓
The issue of 200 units is costed at £1,000	✓		

Task 2.3

Characteristic	True	False
FIFO costs issues of inventory at the most recent purchase prices		✓
AVCO costs issues of inventory at the oldest purchase prices		✓
LIFO costs issues of inventory at the oldest purchase prices		✓
FIFO values closing inventory at the most recent purchase prices	✓	
LIFO values closing inventory at the most recent purchase prices		✓
AVCO values closing inventory at the latest purchase prices		✓

Task 2.4

Method	Cost of Issue on 18 March	Closing Inventory at 31 March
FIFO	£600 + £1,200 + (£2,500/500 × 100) = **£2,300**	£600 + £1,200 + £2,500 – £2,300 + £2,400) = **£4,400**
LIFO	£2,500 + (£1200/300 × 100) = **£2,900**	£600 + £1,200 + £2,500 – £2,900 + £2,400 = **£3,800**
AVCO	[(£600 + £1,200 + £2,500)/1,000] × 600 = **£2,580**	£600 + £1,200 + £2,500 – £2,580 + £2,400 = **£4,120**

Task 2.5

Characteristic	True	False
Direct labour costs can be identified with the goods being made or the service being provided	✓	
Indirect costs vary directly with the level of activity		✓

Task 2.6

Payment method	Time- rate	Piecework	Time-rate plus bonus
Labour is paid based on the production achieved		✓	
Labour is paid extra if an agreed level of output is exceeded			✓
Labour is paid according to hours worked	✓		

Task 2.7

Statement	Time- rate	Piecework	Time-rate plus bonus
An employee is paid £432 for the 36 hours she has worked	✓		
An employee is paid £400 for the 800 units she has produced		✓	
An employee is paid £420 for the 35 hours that she worked and an extra £45 for efficient production			✓

Task 2.8

Worker	Hours worked	Basic wage	Overtime	Gross wage
A. Singh	35 hours	£350	£0	£350
S. Callaghan	40 hours	£350	£75	£425

Task 2.9

Worker	Units produced in week	Gross wage
G. Patel	300 units	£240
A. Jones	400 units	£320

Task 2.10

Worker	Hours worked	Units produced	Basic wage	Bonus	Gross wage
A. Smith	35	150	£420	£0	£420
J. O'Hara	35	175	£420	£0	£420
M. Stizgt	35	210	£420	£35	£455

Task 2.11

	True	False
A variance is the difference between budgeted and actual cost	✓	
A favourable variance means budgeted costs are greater than actual costs	✓	

Task 2.12

Cost Type	Budget £	Actual £	Variance	Adverse	Favourable
Direct materials	38,400	40,100	£1,700	✓	
Direct labour	74,200	73,000	£1,200		✓
Production overheads	68,000	72,100	£4,100	✓	
Administration overheads	52,000	54,900	£2,900	✓	
Selling and distribution overheads	43,000	41,900	£1,100		✓

Task 2.13

Cost Type	Budget	Variance	Actual cost £	Significant	Not Significant
Direct materials	£75,100	£6,000 (F)	69,100		✓
Direct labour	£64,500	£5,250 (A)	69,750	✓	
Production overheads	£33,800	£2,600 (A)	36,400		✓
Administration overheads	£24,300	£1,900 (F)	22,400		✓
Selling and distribution overheads	£27,400	£2,250 (A)	29,650	✓	

Task 2.14

Variance	Relevant manager
Direct materials	Purchasing manager OR Production manager
Production overheads	Production manager

AAT PRACTICE ASSESSMENT 2
BASIC COSTING

Time allowed: 2 hours

AAT PRACTICE
ASSESSMENT 2

Basic Costing AAT practice assessment 2

Section 1

Task 1.1

Listed in the table below are some of the characteristics of financial accounting and management accounting systems.

Indicate whether the following characteristics describe EITHER financial accounting OR management accounting.

Characteristic	Financial accounting	Management accounting
Its output is accounts that will be used by shareholders		
It is a system that produces information that helps managers to manage		
It uses historic cost to produce statements for external publication		
It uses cost behaviour as a classification to determine cost per unit		

Task 1.2

Downside Ltd is an engineering company.

Classify each of the following costs by element (materials, labour or overheads) by putting a tick in the relevant column of the table below.

Cost	Materials	Labour	Overheads
Steel used in manufacturing			
Wages of production workers			
Fees of external accountant			
Factory cleaning costs			

Task 1.3

Helcot Ltd is a manufacturer of helicopters.

Classify each of the following costs by nature (direct or indirect) by putting a tick in the relevant column of the table below.

Cost	Direct	Indirect
Wages paid to production line workers		
Polycarbonate sheeting used in the manufacture of helicopter windows		
Heating costs of factory		
Purchasing department costs to place orders		

Task 1.4

Mulligan Ltd is a manufacturer of golf clubs.

Classify the following costs incurred by function (production, administration, selling and distribution, or finance) by putting a tick in the relevant column of the table below.

Cost	Production	Administration	Selling and Distribution	Finance
Metal used to make the golf clubs				
Fuel used by delivery lorries				
Promotion event at a golf exhibition				
Salaries of office staff				

Task 1.5

Downside Ltd is an engineering company.

Classify each of the following costs by their behaviour (fixed, variable, or semi-variable) by putting a tick in the relevant column of the table below.

Cost	Fixed	Variable	Semi-variable
Steel used in manufacturing			
Production workers paid on a time rate and bonus method			
Machinery maintenance costs based upon usage			
Insurance costs for factory			

Task 1.6

Hillman Ltd, a hotel group, uses a numerical coding structure and extracts from one profit centre and three cost centres are outlined below. Each code has a sub-code so each transaction will be coded as ***/***. So, for example, an indirect room cost would be coded 210/202.

You are required to classify the revenue and expense transactions shown in the transaction column of the table below using the code column for your answer.

Profit/Cost centre	Cost code	Sub-classification	Sub-code	Transaction	Code
Sales	100	Room sales	101	Revenue from room booking	/
		Restaurant sales	102	Breakfast sales in the restaurant	/
Restaurant	200	Direct cost	201	Laundry costs of towels used in the sports centre	/
		Indirect cost	202	Salary of restaurant manager	/
Rooms	210	Direct cost	201	Purchase of food for restaurant	/
		Indirect cost	202	Maintenance costs of hotel rooms	/
Sports Centre	220	Direct cost	201		
		Indirect cost	202		

Task 1.7

Greendrop Ltd manufactures and sells footwear. It uses a coding system for its elements of cost (materials, labour or overheads) and then further classifies each element by nature (direct or indirect cost) as below. So, for example, the code for direct materials is A101.

You are required to classify the costs listed in the cost column of the table below using the code column for your answer.

Element of cost	Cost	Nature of cost	Sub-code	Cost	Code
Material	A	Direct	101	Material used for shoe laces	
		Indirect	106	Wages of canteen staff	
Labour	B	Direct	101	Shoeboxes used for every pair of shoes sold	
		Indirect	106	Electricity costs for shops	
Overheads	C	Direct	101	Wages for staff on assembly line	
		Indirect	106		

Task 1.8

Identify the type of cost behaviour (fixed, variable or semi-variable) described by each statement below by putting a tick in the relevant column of the table below.

Statement	Fixed	Variable	Semi-variable
At 600 units costs are £4 per unit and at 800 units costs are £3 per unit			
At 1,500 unit costs are £5,000 made up of a fixed element of £2,000 and a cost of £2 a unit			
Costs are £3,000 for 1,000 units and £4,200 for 1,400 units			

Task 1.9

Classify the following costs as either fixed or variable by putting a tick in the relevant column of the table below.

Cost	Fixed	Variable
Bonus paid to production workers based upon output		
Salary of the Purchasing Department manager		
Material used in production		
Commission paid to sales team based on sales made		

Task 1.10

Complete the table below showing fixed costs, variable costs, total costs and unit cost at the different levels of production. You are told that fixed costs are £120,000 and that variable costs are £150 per unit.

Units	Fixed costs £	Variable costs £	Total costs £	Unit cost £
2,000				
2,400				
4,000				

Task 1.11

Wellington Ltd is costing a single product which has the following cost details for a production level of 40,000 units:

Variable costs per unit

Materials	£500 per 100 units
Labour	£8.00 per hour and one unit of the product takes 30 minutes to produce
Total fixed costs	£240,000

Complete the following total cost and unit cost table for a production level of 40,000 units.

Element of cost	Total cost £	Unit cost £
Materials		
Labour		
Overheads		
Total		

Task 1.12

Greymouth Ltd makes a single product and for a production level of 25,000 units has the following cost details:

Materials	12,500 kilos	at £20 per kilo
Labour	10,000 kilos	at £15 an hour
Total fixed costs		£275,000

Complete the table below to show the unit cost at the production level of 25,000 units.

Element of cost	Unit cost £
Materials	
Labour	
Overheads	
Total	

Section 2

Task 2.1

Reorder the following costs into a manufacturing account format for the year ended 31 December. You should drag each item to the position where you want it to be in the list on the right side of the table below and then drop it into place.

Costs		Manufacturing account
Closing inventory of raw materials	£60,000	
COST OF GOODS MANUFACTURED	£1,170,000	
Purchases of raw materials	£300,000	
MANUFACTURING COST	£1,182,000	
Manufacturing overheads	£318,000	
DIRECT MATERIALS USED	£282,000	
COST OF GOODS SOLD	£1,200,000	
Direct labour	£582,000	
Opening inventory of work in progress	£48,000	
Opening inventory of finished goods	£180,000	
PRIME COST	£864,000	
Closing inventory of finished goods	£150,000	
Closing inventory of work in progress	£60,000	
Opening inventory of raw materials	£42,000	

Task 2.2

You are told the opening inventory of a single raw material in the stores is 600 units at £6 per unit. During the month, a receipt of 300 units at £9 per unit is received and the following week 400 units are issued.

Identify the valuation method described in the statements below.

Statement	FIFO	LIFO	AVCO
The issue of 400 units is costed at £2,800			
The closing inventory is valued at £3,000			
The issue of 400 units is costed at £3,300			

Task 2.3

Identify the following statements as True or False by putting a tick in the relevant column of the table below.

Statement	True	False
FIFO costs issues of inventories at the oldest purchase price		
AVCO costs issue of inventories at the oldest purchase price		
LIFO costs issues of inventories at the oldest purchase price		
FIFO values closing inventories at the most recent purchase price		
LIFO values closing inventories at the most recent purchase price		
AVCO values closing inventories at the average purchase price		

Task 2.4

Wellington Ltd has the following movements in a certain type of inventory into and out its stores for the month of May:

DATE	RECEIPTS		ISSUES	
	Units	Cost	Units	Cost
May 4	200	£800		
May 9	350	£1,575		
May 13	450	£2,250		
May 19			800	
May 26	400	£1,800		

Complete the table below by entering the cost of issue and closing inventory values.

Method	Cost of issue 19 May £	Closing inventory 31 May £
FIFO		
LIFO		
AVCO		

Task 2.5

Identify the following statements as True or False by putting a tick in the relevant column of the table below.

Statement	True	False
Direct labour costs can be associated with the product made		
Indirect labour costs will always be fixed costs		

Task 2.6

Identify the labour payment method by putting a tick in the relevant column of the table below.

Payment method	Time-rate	Piecework	Time-rate plus bonus
Labour will be rewarded beyond a guaranteed wage if they are efficient			
Labour will be paid the same regardless of output if their attendance is the same			
If a worker produces less then they will be paid less			

Task 2.7

Identify the labour payment method described in the following statements by putting a tick in the relevant column of the table below.

Statement	Time-rate	Piecework	Time-rate plus bonus
An employee is paid £350 for her week's production of 700 units at £0.50 per unit			
An employee works for 30 hours at £12 per hour and is paid £360			
An employee works for 35 hours at £10 per hour and is paid £350 plus an extra £50 for efficient production			

Task 2.8

Helcot Ltd pays a time rate of £15 per hour to its direct labour force for a standard 38 hour week. Any of the labour force working in excess of 38 hours is paid an overtime rate of £25 per hour.

Calculate the basic wage, overtime and gross wage for the week for the two employees in the table below. Note: if no overtime is paid you should enter 0 as the overtime for that employee.

Employee	Hours worked	Basic wage £	Overtime £	Gross wage £
J. Smyth	42			
S. Khan	45			

Task 2.9

Downside Ltd uses a piecework method to pay labour in one of its factories.
The rate used is £11 per 10 units produced.

Calculate the gross wage for the week for the two workers in the table below.

Employee	Unites produced in week	Gross wage £
J. Green	550	
W. White	670	

Task 2.10

Greymouth Ltd uses a time rate method with bonus to pay its direct labour force in one of its factories. The time rate used is £13 per hour and a worker is expected to produce 12 units an hour. Anything over this and the worker is paid a bonus of £0.40 per unit.

Calculate the gross wage for the week including bonus for the three workers in the table below. Note: if no bonus is paid you should enter 0 as the bonus for that employee in the table.

Employee	Hours worked	Units produced	Basic wage £	Bonus £	Gross wage £
E. O'Kane	43	556			
B. Roberts	39	351			
P. Fletcher	37	504			

Task 2.11

Identify the following statements as True or False by putting a tick in the relevant column of the table below.

Statement	True	False
A favourable variance means actual cost is greater than budgeted cost		
A cost variance is the difference between actual cost and budgeted cost		

Task 2.12

Wellington Ltd has produced a performance report detailing budgeted and actual costs for last month.

Calculate the amount of the variance for each cost type and then determine whether it is adverse or favourable by putting a tick in the relevant column of the table below.

Cost type	Budget £	Actual £	Variance £	Adverse	Favourable
Direct materials	49,200	47,600			
Direct labour	67,400	66,300			
Production overheads	87,200	84,200			
Administration overheads	47,100	56,200			
Selling and distribution overheads	29,700	28,100			

Task 2.13

The following performance report for last month has been produced for Pensarn Ltd as summarised in the table below. Any variance in excess of 5% of budget is deemed to be significant and should be reported to the relevant manager for review and appropriate action.

Examine the adverse (A) and favourable (F) variances in the table below and calculate the actual cost, indicating whether each variance is significant or not significant by putting a tick in the relevant column of the table below.

Cost type	Budget £	Variance £	Actual cost £	Significant	Not significant
Direct materials	46,200	2,350 (F)			
Direct labour	37,350	1,290 (A)			
Production overheads	22,850	1,200 (A)			
Administration overheads	16,320	920 (A)			
Selling and distribution overheads	15,390	740 (A)			

Task 2.14

It was noted from the performance report for Towan Ltd for last month that the following cost variances were significant:

- Direct labour
- Direct materials

These cost variances need to be reported to the relevant manager for review and action if required.

Identify, for the following significant cost variances, one relevant manager to whom the performance report should be sent.

Cost variance	Relevant manager
Direct labour	▼
Direct materials	▼

Picklist:

Administration manager
Distribution manager
Finance manager
Human resources manager
Production manager
Product development manager
Purchasing manager
Research manager
Sales manager
Transport manager

AAT PRACTICE ASSESSMENT 2
BASIC COSTING

ANSWERS

Basic Costing AAT practice assessment 2

Section 1

Task 1.1

Characteristics	Financial accounting	Management accounting
Its output is accounts that will be used by shareholders	✓	
It is a system that produces information that helps managers to manage		✓
It uses historic cost to produce statements for external publication	✓	
It uses cost behaviour as a classification to determine per unit		✓

Task 1.2

Cost	Materials	Labour	Overheads
Steel used in manufacturing	✓		
Wages of production workers		✓	
Fees of external accountant			✓
Factory cleaning costs			✓

Task 1.3

Cost	Direct	Indirect
Wages paid to production line workers	✓	
Polycarbonate sheeting used in the manufacture of helicopter windows	✓	
Heating costs of factory		✓
Purchasing department costs to place orders		✓

Task 1.4

Cost	Production	Administration	Selling and Distribution	Finance
Metal used to make the golf clubs	✓			
Fuel used by delivery lorries			✓	
Promotion event at a golf exhibition			✓	
Salaries of office staff		✓		

Task 1.5

Cost	Fixed	Variable	Semi-variable
Steel used in manufacturing		✓	
Production workers paid on a time rate and bonus method			✓
Machinery maintenance costs based upon usage		✓	
Insurance costs for factory	✓		

Task 1.6

Transaction	Code
Revenue from room booking	100/101
Breakfast sales in the restaurant	100/102
Laundry costs of towels used in the sports centre	220/202
Salary of restaurant manager	200/202
Purchase of food for restaurant	200/201
Maintenance costs of hotel rooms	210/202

Task 1.7

Cost	Code
Material used for shoe laces	A101
Wages of canteen staff	B106
Shoeboxes used for every pair of shoes sold	A101
Electricity costs for shops	C106
Wages for staff on assembly line	B101

Task 1.8

Statement	Fixed	Variable	Semi-variable
At 600 units costs are £4 per unit and at 800 units costs are £3 per unit	✓		
At 1,500 units costs are £5,000 made up of a fixed element of £2,000 and a cost £2 a unit			✓
Costs are £3,000 for 1,000 units and £4,200 for 1,400 units		✓	

Task 1.9

Cost	Fixed	Variable
Bonus paid to production workers based upon output		✓
Salary of the Purchasing Department manager	✓	
Material used in production		✓
Commission paid to sales team based on sales made		✓

Task 1.10

Units	Fixed costs £	Variable costs £	Total costs £	Unit cost £
2,000	120,000	300,000	420,000	210
2,400	120,000	360,000	480,000	200
4,000	120,000	600,000	720,000	180

Task 1.11

Element of cost	Total cost £	Unit cost £
Materials	200,000	5
Labour	160,000	4
Overheads	240,000	6
Total	600,000	15

Task 1.12

Element of cost	Unit cost £
Materials	10
Labour	6
Overheads	11
Total	27

Section 2

Task 2.1

Costs		Manufacturing account	
Closing inventory of raw materials	£60,000	Opening inventory of raw materials	£42,000
COST OF GOODS MANUFACTURED	£1,170,000	Purchases or raw materials	£300,000
Purchases of raw materials	£300,000	Closing inventory of raw materials	£60,000
MANUFACTURING COST	£1,182,000	DIRECT MATERIALS USED	£282,000
Manufacturing overheads	£318,000	Direct labour	£582,000
DIRECT MATERIALS USED	£282,000	PRIME COST	£864,000
COST OF GOODS SOLD	£1,200,000	Manufacturing overheads	£318,000
Direct labour	£582,000	MANUFACTURING COST	£1,182,000
Opening inventory of work in progress	£48,000	Opening inventory of work in progress	£48,000
Opening inventory of finished goods	£180,000	Closing inventory of work in progress	£60,000
PRIME COST	£864,000	COST OF GOODS MANUFACTURED	£1,170,000
Closing inventory of finished goods	£150,000	Opening inventory of finished goods	£180,000
Closing inventory of work in progress	£60,000	Closing inventory of finished goods	£150,000
Opening inventory of raw materials	£42,000	COST OF GOODS SOLD	£1,200,000

Task 2.2

Statement	FIFO	LIFO	AVCO
The issue of 400 units costed at £2,800			✓
The closing inventory is valued at £3,000		✓	
The issue of 400 units is costed at £3,300		✓	

Task 2.3

Statement	True	False
FIFO costs issues of inventories at the oldest purchase price	✓	
AVCO costs issue of inventories at the oldest purchase price		✓
LIFO costs issues of inventories at the oldest purchase price		✓
FIFO values closing inventories at the most recent purchase price	✓	
LIFO values closing inventories at the most recent purchase price		✓
AVCO values closing inventories at the average purchase price	✓	

Task 2.4

Method	Cost of issue 19 May £	Closing inventory 31 May £
FIFO	£800 + £1,575 + (250/450 × £2,250) = **3,625**	£1,800 + (200/450 × £2,250) = **2,800**
LIFO	£2,250 + £1,575 = **3,825**	£1,800 + £800 = **2,600**
AVCO	[(£800 + £1,575 + £2,250)/1,000] × 800 = **3,700**	£800 + £1,575 + £2,250 – £3,700 + £1,800 = **2,725**

Task 2.5

Statement	True	False
Direct labour costs can be associated with the product made	✓	
Indirect labour costs will always be fixed costs		✓

Task 2.6

Payment method	Time-rate	Piecework	Time-rate plus bonus
Labour will be rewarded beyond a guaranteed wage if they are efficient			✓
Labour will be paid the same regardless of output if their attendance is the same	✓		
If a worker produces less then they will be paid less		✓	

Task 2.7

Statement	Time-rate	Piecework	Time-rate plus bonus
An employee is paid £350 for her week's production of 700 units at £0.50 per unit		✓	
An employee works for 30 hours at £12 per hour and is paid £360	✓		
An employee works for 35 hours at £10 per hour and is paid £350 plus an extra £50 for efficient production			✓

Task 2.8

Employee	Hours worked	Basic wage £	Overtime £	Gross wage £
J. Smyth	42	570	100	670
S. Khan	45	570	175	745

Task 2.9

Employee	Unites produced in week	Gross wage £
J. Green	550	605
W. White	670	737

Task 2.10

Employee	Hours worked	Units produced	Basic wage £	Bonus £	Gross wage £
E. O'Kane	43	556	559	16	575
B. Roberts	39	351	507	0	507
P. Fletcher	37	504	481	24	505

Task 2.11

Statement	True	False
A favourable variance means actual cost is greater than budget cost.		✓
A cost variance is the difference between actual cost and budgeted cost.	✓	

Task 2.12

Cost type	Budget £	Actual £	Variance £	Adverse	Favourable
Direct materials	49,200	47,600	1,600		✓
Direct labour	67,400	66,300	1,100		✓
Production overheads	87,200	84,200	3,000		✓
Administration overheads	47,100	56,200	9,100	✓	
Selling and distribution overheads	29,700	28,100	1,600		✓

Task 2.13

Cost type	Budget £	Variance £	Actual cost £	Significant	Not significant
Direct materials	46,200	2,350 (F)	43,850	✓	
Direct labour	37,350	1,290 (A)	38,640		✓
Production overheads	22,850	1,200 (A)	24,050	✓	
Administration overheads	16,320	920 (A)	17,240	✓	
Selling and distribution overheads	15,390	740 (A)	16,130		✓

Task 2.14

Cost variance	Relevant manager
Direct labour	Human resources OR Production manager
Direct materials	Purchasing OR Production manager

BPP PRACTICE ASSESSMENT 1
BASIC COSTING

Time allowed: 2 hours

Basic Costing BPP practice assessment 1

Section 1

Task 1.1

The table below lists some of the characteristics of manufacturing, retail and service organisations.

Indicate a characteristic for each organisation by putting a tick in the relevant column of the table below.

Characteristic	Retail	Manufacturing	Service
Doesn't manufacture or sell a physical product			
Buys in ready made goods to sell			
Buys in raw materials			

Task 1.2

Dartmouth Ltd is a manufacturer of garden gnomes.

Classify the following costs by element (materials, labour or overheads) by putting a tick in the relevant column of the table below.

Cost	Materials	Labour	Overheads
Salary of the accounts manager			
Wages of employees painting the gnomes			
Electricity in the workshops			
Plaster used in making the gnomes			

Task 1.3

Totnes Ltd is in business as a beauty salon.

Classify the following costs by nature (direct or indirect) by putting a tick in the relevant column of the table below.

Cost	Direct	Indirect
Nail polish used on nails		
Rent and rates for salon		
Wages of security guard		
Wages of beauticians		

Task 1.4

Barnstaple Ltd produces surfboards.

Classify the following costs by function (production, administration, or selling and distribution) by putting a tick in the relevant column of the table below.

Cost	Production	Administration	Selling and Distribution
Purchases of fibreglass for the boards			
Cost of delivering finished boards to surf shops			
Salaries of board waxers			
Fees for monthly bookkeeper			

Task 1.5

Exmouth Ltd is a manufacturer of tweed cloth.

Classify the following costs by their behaviour (fixed, variable, or semi-variable) by putting a tick in the relevant column of the table below.

Cost	Fixed	Variable	Semi-variable
Labour costs paid on a piecework basis			
Spun wool used in making the cloth			
Marketing cost for the year			
Telephone costs for the sales staff that include a standing charge			

Task 1.6

Bovey Ltd makes tractors. It uses a alpha-numerical coding structure based on one profit centre and three cost centres as outlined below. Each code has a sub-code so each transaction will be coded as */***.

Profit/Cost centre	Code	Sub-classification	Sub-code
Sales	A	UK sales	100
		Overseas sales	200
Production	B	Direct cost	100
		Indirect cost	200
Administration	C	Direct cost	100
		Indirect cost	200
Selling and Distribution	D	Direct cost	100
		Indirect cost	200

Code the following revenue and expense transactions, which have been extracted from purchase invoices, sales invoices and payroll, using the table below.

Transaction	Code
Paint for tractors	
Sales to Tyneside	
Factory rates	
Sales to Germany	
Insurance on the upstairs offices	
Maintenance contract for production machinery	

Task 1.7

Torbay Limited operates a dog grooming parlour and uses a coding system for its elements of cost (materials, labour or overheads) and then further classifies each element by nature (direct or indirect cost) as below. So, for example, the code for direct materials is 1/100.

Element of cost	Code	Nature of cost	Code
Materials	1	Direct	100
		Indirect	200
Labour	2	Direct	100
		Indirect	200
Overheads	3	Direct	100
		Indirect	200

Code the following costs, extracted from invoices and payroll, using the table below.

Cost	Code
Shampoo used on the dogs	
Fees for solicitors to negotiate rent reduction on parlour	
Salary of dog groomer	
Wages of receptionist	
Carpet shampoo used by salon cleaner	

Task 1.8

Identify the following statements as either True or False by putting a tick in the relevant column of the table below.

	True	False
Fixed costs never change		
Variable costs change with output levels		
Semi-variable costs show a step increase at a particular level of output		

Task 1.9

Plustyre Ltd fixes cars and makes sure they are valeted so they are returned to their owners in a perfect state.

Classify the following costs as either fixed or variable by putting a tick in the relevant column of the table below.

Costs	Fixed	Variable
Valets paid at piecework rate for each car valeted		
Hourly wages of mechanics paid for each car fixed		
Salaries of supervisors		
Rent for the workshop used to fix cars		

Task 1.10

Complete the table below showing fixed costs, variable costs, total costs and unit cost at the different levels of production.

Units	Fixed costs	Variable costs	Total costs	Unit cost
2,000	£30,000	£15,000	£45,000	£22.50
5,000	£	£	£	£
10,000	£	£	£	£
15,000	£	£	£	£

Task 1.11

Torre Ltd is costing a single product, which has the following cost details:

Variable costs per unit

Materials	£5
Labour	£6
Total fixed costs	£100,000

Complete the following total cost and unit cost table for a production level of 10,000 units.

Element	Total cost	Unit cost
Material	£	£
Labour	£	£
Overheads	£	£
Total	£	£

Task 1.12

Kingswear Ltd makes a single product and for a production level of 20,000 units has the following cost details:

Materials	5,000 kilos at	£10 per kilo
Labour	4,000 hours at	£15 an hour
Overheads		£50,000

Complete the table below to show the unit cost at the production level of 20,000 units.

Element	Unit cost
Material	£
Labour	£
Overheads	£
Total	£

Section 2

Task 2.1

Reorder the following headings and costs into a manufacturing account format on the right side of the table below for the year ended 31 December.

	£	Manufacturing account	£
Closing inventory of work in progress	25,000		
Direct labour	242,500		
Opening inventory of raw materials	17,500		
Closing inventory of finished goods	62,500		
Closing inventory of raw materials	25,000		
Manufacturing overheads	132,500		
COST OF GOODS SOLD	500,000		
MANUFACTURING COST	492,500		
Purchases of raw materials	125,000		
Opening inventory of work in progress	20,000		
Opening inventory of finished goods	75,000		
PRIME COST	360,000		
DIRECT MATERIALS USED	117,500		
COST OF GOODS MANUFACTURED	487,500		

Task 2.2

Identify the correct inventory valuation method from the characteristic given by putting a tick in the relevant column of the table below.

Characteristic	FIFO	LIFO	AVCO
Inventory is valued at the most recent purchase cost			
Issues are valued at the average of the cost of purchases			
Issues are valued at the most recent purchase cost			

Task 2.3

Identify whether the following statements are True or False by putting a tick in the relevant column of the table below.

	True	False
AVCO values closing inventory at the most recent purchase price		
LIFO values closing inventory at the most recent purchase price		
FIFO values closing inventory at the most recent purchase price		
AVCO costs issues of inventory at the oldest purchase price		
LIFO costs issues of inventory at the oldest purchase price		
FIFO costs issues of inventory at the oldest purchase price		

Task 2.4

Jersey Ltd has the following movements in a certain type of inventory into and out of its stores for the month of May:

DATE	RECEIPTS		ISSUES	
	Units	Cost	Units	Cost
May 5	500	£1,500		
May 8	750	£3,000		
May 12	1,250	£6,250		
May 18			1,500	
May 25	1,000	£6,000		

Complete the table below for the issue and closing inventory values.

Method	Cost of issue on 18 May	Closing inventory at 31 May
FIFO	£	£
LIFO	£	£
AVCO	£	£

Task 2.5

Identify the following statements as True or False by putting a tick in the relevant column of the table below.

	True	False
The variable cost per unit rises with the level of output		
Overheads vary in line with output		

Task 2.6

Identify the labour payment method by putting a tick in the relevant column of the table below.

Payment method	Time- rate	Piecework	Time-rate plus bonus
An amount is paid for each unit or task successfully completed			
A basic amount is paid per hour worked			
If output exceeds a preset level an incentive is paid in addition to hourly rate			

Task 2.7

Identify one advantage for each labour payment method by putting a tick in the relevant column of the table below.

Payment method	Time- rate	Piecework
Pay remains the same even when output fluctuates due to demand		
Easy to calculate an employee's pay		
More efficient workers are paid more		

Task 2.8

Cardiff Ltd pays a time-rate of £15 per hour to its direct labour for a standard 35-hour week. Any of the labour force working in excess of 35 hours is paid an overtime rate of £25 per hour.

Calculate the gross wage for the week for the two workers in the table below.

Worker	Hours worked	Basic wage	Overtime	Gross wage
J Edwards	35 hours	£	£	£
L Rakowski	41 hours	£	£	£

Task 2.9

Swansea Ltd uses a piecework method to pay labour in one of its factories. The rate used is 70p per unit produced.

Calculate the gross wage for the week for the two workers in the table below.

Worker	Units produced in week	Gross wage
G Gently	350 units	£
A Ransome	390 units	£

Task 2.10

Brecon Ltd uses a time-rate method with bonus to pay its direct labour in one of its factories. The time-rate used is £15 per hour and a worker is expected to produce five units an hour, anything over this and the worker is paid a bonus of £1.50 per unit.

Calculate the gross wage for the week including bonus for the three workers in the table below.

Worker	Hours worked	Units produced	Basic wage	Bonus	Gross wage
R Butler	35	160	£	£	£
S Douglas	35	155	£	£	£
L Howard	35	200	£	£	£

Task 2.11

Identify the following statements as being True or False by putting a tick in the relevant column of the table below.

	True	False
All variances should be treated as significant and be fully investigated		
An adverse variance means budgeted costs are lower than actual costs		

Task 2.12

Merthyr Ltd has produced a performance report detailing budgeted and actual cost for last month.

Calculate the amount of the variance for each cost type and then determine whether it is adverse or favourable by typing F for favourable and A for adverse in the right hand column of the table below.

Cost type	Budget £	Actual £	Variance	Adverse/Favourable
Direct materials	40,500	40,200	£	
Direct labour	75,000	73,125	£	
Production overheads	70,000	72,120	£	
Administration overheads	55,000	54,950	£	
Selling and Distribution overheads	45,000	42,950	£	

Task 2.13

A performance report for this month has been produced for Ambleside Ltd as summarised in the table below. Any variance in excess of 10% of budget is deemed to be significant and should be reported to the relevant manager for review and appropriate action.

Examine the variances in the table below and indicate whether they are significant or not significant by typing S for significant and NS for not significant in the right-hand column below.

Cost type	Budget	Variance	Adverse/ Favourable	Significant/ Not significant
Direct materials	£35,000	£3,335	Adverse	
Direct labour	£70,000	£8,015	Adverse	
Production overheads	£65,000	£4,208	Favourable	
Administration overheads	£54,000	£5,980	Adverse	
Selling and Distribution overheads	£42,000	£1,150	Adverse	

Task 2.14

It was noted from the performance report for Ambleside Ltd for an earlier month that the following cost variances were significant:

- Direct material cost
- Selling overheads

These variances needed to be reported to the relevant managers for review and appropriate action if required.

Identify a relevant manager for each significant variance to whom the performance report should be sent.

Variance	Relevant manager
Direct material cost	▼
Administration overheads	▼

Picklist:

Production manager
Sales manager
HR manager
Administration manager

BPP PRACTICE ASSESSMENT 1
BASIC COSTING

ANSWERS

Basic Costing BPP practice assessment 1

Section 1

Task 1.1

Characteristic	Retail	Manufacturing	Service
Doesn't manufacture or sell a physical product			✓
Buys in ready made goods to sell	✓		
Buys in raw materials		✓	

Task 1.2

Cost	Materials	Labour	Overheads
Salary of the accounts manager			✓
Wages of employees painting the gnomes		✓	
Electricity in the workshops			✓
Plaster used in making the gnomes	✓		

Task 1.3

Cost	Direct	Indirect
Wages of beauticians	✓	
Wages of security guard		✓
Rent and rates for salon		✓
Nail polish used on nails	✓	

Task 1.4

Cost	Production	Administration	Selling and Distribution
Purchases of fibreglass for the boards	✓		
Cost of delivering finished boards to surf shops			✓
Salaries of board waxers	✓		
Fees for monthly bookkeeper		✓	

Task 1.5

Cost	Fixed	Variable	Semi-variable
Labour costs paid on a piecework basis		✓	
Spun wool used in making the cloth		✓	
Marketing cost for the year	✓		
Telephone costs for the sales staff that include a standing charge			✓

Task 1.6

Transaction	Code
Paint for tractors	B/100
Sales to Tyneside	A/100
Factory rates	B/200
Sales to Germany	A/200
Insurance on the upstairs offices	C/200
Maintenance contract for production machinery	B/200

Task 1.7

Cost	Code
Shampoo used on the dogs	1/100
Fees for solicitors to negotiate rent reduction on parlour	3/200
Salary of dog groomer	2/100
Wages of receptionist	2/200
Carpet shampoo used by salon cleaner	1/200

Task 1.8

	True	False
Fixed costs never change		✓
Variable costs change with output levels	✓	
Semi-variable costs show a step increase at a particular level of output		✓

Task 1.9

Costs	Fixed	Variable
Valets paid at piecework rate for each car valeted		✓
Hourly wages of mechanics paid for each car fixed		✓
Salaries of supervisors	✓	
Rent for the workshop used to fix cars	✓	

Task 1.10

Units	Fixed costs	Variable costs	Total costs	Unit cost
2,000	£30,000	£15,000	£45,000	£22.50
5,000	£30,000	£37,500	£67,500	£13.50
10,000	£30,000	£75,000	£105,000	£10.50
15,000	£30,000	£112,500	£142,500	£9.50

Task 1.11

Element	Total cost	Unit cost
Material	£50,000	£5.00
Labour	£60,000	£6.00
Overheads	£100,000	£10.00
Total	£210,000	£21.00

Task 1.12

Element	Unit cost
Material	£2.50
Labour	£3.00
Overheads	£2.50
Total	£8.00

Section 2

Task 2.1

Costs	£	Manufacturing account	£
Closing inventory of work in progress	25,000	Opening inventory of raw materials	17,500
Direct labour	242,500	Purchases of raw materials	125,000
Opening inventory of raw materials	17,500	Closing inventory of raw materials	25,000
Closing inventory of finished goods	62,500	DIRECT MATERIALS USED	117,500
Closing inventory of raw materials	25,000	Direct labour	242,500
Manufacturing overheads	132,500	PRIME COST	360,000
COST OF GOODS SOLD	500,000	Manufacturing overheads	132,500
MANUFACTURING COST	492,500	MANUFACTURING COST	492,500
Purchases of raw materials	125,000	Opening inventory of work in progress	20,000
Opening inventory of work in Progress	20,000	Closing inventory of work in Progress	25,000
Opening inventory of finished goods	75,000	COST OF GOODS MANUFACTURED	487,500
PRIME COST	360,000	Opening inventory of finished goods	75,000
DIRECT MATERIALS USED	117,500	Closing inventory of finished goods	62,500
COST OF GOODS MANUFACTURED	487,500	COST OF GOODS SOLD	500,000

Task 2.2

Characteristic	FIFO	LIFO	AVCO
Inventory is valued at the most recent purchase cost	✓		
Issues are valued at the average of the cost of purchases			✓
Issues are valued at the most recent purchase cost		✓	

Task 2.3

	True	False
AVCO values closing inventory at the most recent purchase price		✓
LIFO values closing inventory at the most recent purchase price		✓
FIFO values closing inventory at the most recent purchase price	✓	
AVCO costs issues of inventory at the oldest purchase price		✓
LIFO costs issues of inventory at the oldest purchase price		✓
FIFO costs issues of inventory at the oldest purchase price	✓	

Task 2.4

Method	Cost of issue on 18 May	Closing inventory at 31 May
FIFO	1,500 + 3,000 + (250/1,250 × 6,250) = £5,750	6,000 + (1,000/1,250 × 6,250) = £11,000
LIFO	6,250 + (250/750 × 3,000) = £7,250	1,500 + (500/750 × 3,000) + 6,000 = £9,500
AVCO	[(1,500 + 3,000 + 6,250)/2,500]× 1,500 = £6,450	[(1,500 + 3,000 + 6,250)/2,500] × 1,000 + 6,000 = £10,300

Task 2.5

	True	False
The variable cost per unit rises with the level of output		✓
Overheads vary in line with output		✓

Task 2.6

Payment method	Time- rate	Piecework	Time-rate plus bonus
An amount is paid for each unit or task successfully completed		✓	
A basic amount is paid per hour worked	✓		
If output exceeds a preset level an incentive is paid in addition to hourly rate			✓

Task 2.7

Payment method	Time- rate	Piecework
Pay remains the same even when output fluctuates due to demand	✓	
Easy to calculate an employee's pay	✓	
More efficient workers are paid more		✓

Task 2.8

Worker	Hours worked	Basic wage	Overtime	Gross wage
J Edwards	35 hours	£525	£0	£525
L Rakowski	41 hours	£525	£150	£675

Task 2.9

Worker	Units produced in week	Gross wage
G Gently	350 units	£245
A Ransome	390 units	£273

Task 2.10

Worker	Hours worked	Units produced	Basic wage	Bonus	Gross wage
R Butler	35	160	£525.00	£0.00	£525.00
S Douglas	35	155	£525.00	£0.00	£525.00
L Howard	35	200	£525.00	£37.50	£562.50

Task 2.11

	True	False
All variances should be treated as significant and fully investigated		✓
An adverse variance means budgeted costs are lower than actual costs	✓	

Task 2.12

Cost type	Budget £	Actual £	Variance	Adverse/Favourable
Direct materials	40,500	40,200	£300	F
Direct labour	75,000	73,125	£1,875	F
Production overheads	70,000	72,120	£2,120	A
Administration overheads	55,000	54,950	£50	F
Selling and Distribution overheads	45,000	42,950	£2,050	F

Task 2.13

Cost type	Budget	Variance	Adverse/ Favourable	Significant/ Not significant
Direct materials	£35,000	£3,335	Adverse	NS
Direct labour	£70,000	£8,015	Adverse	S
Production overheads	£65,000	£4,208	Favourable	NS
Administration overheads	£54,000	£5,980	Adverse	S
Selling and Distribution overheads	£42,000	£1,150	Adverse	NS

Task 2.14

Variance	Relevant manager
Direct material cost	Production manager
Selling overheads	Sales manager

BPP PRACTICE ASSESSMENT 2
BASIC COSTING

Time allowed: 2 hours

PRACTICE ASSESSMENT 2

Basic Costing – BPP practice assessment 2

Section 1

Task 1.1

The table below lists some typical business transactions.

Indicate whether each one is capital or revenue by putting a tick in the relevant column.

Transaction	Capital	Revenue
Purchase of office furniture for office manager		
Purchase of office furniture by office furniture saleroom for resale		
Paying VAT		
Making cash sales		

Task 1.2

Ambleside Ltd makes walking boots.

Classify the following costs by element (materials, labour or overheads) by putting a tick in the relevant column of the table below.

Cost	Materials	Labour	Overheads
Rent and rates on the workshop			
Leather for making the boots			
Salary of bookkeeper employed in the business			
Wages of two cobblers making lasts for the boots			

Task 1.3

Windermere Ltd is in business as a health spa and resort hotel.

Classify the following costs by nature (direct or indirect) by putting a tick in the relevant column of the table below.

Cost	Direct	Indirect
Supplies of food bought in for the kitchen		
Interest on mortgage to buy the hotel		
Hotel cashier's salary		
Wages of waiters in the hotel restaurant		

Task 1.4

Derwentwater Ltd makes dinghies.

Classify the following costs by function (production, administration, or selling and distribution) by putting a tick in the relevant column of the table below.

Cost	Production	Administration	Selling and Distribution
Advertising dinghies in local newspaper			
Material for making sails in the factory			
Fees to estate agent for locating new premises			
Salaries of seamstresses stitching material for sails			

Task 1.5

Bassenthwaite Ltd is a pottery making bowls and cups.

Classify the following costs by their behaviour (fixed, variable, or semi-variable) by putting a tick in the relevant column of the table below.

Cost	Fixed	Variable	Semi-variable
Charge for electricity for the kilns firing the pots that includes a standing charge			
Annual entertainment budget for the pottery			
Cost of glazes bought in to glaze the pots			
Labour costs for potters paid on a piecework basis			

Task 1.6

Carlisle Ltd makes drills for use by dentists. It uses an alpha-numeric coding structure based on one profit centre and three cost centres as outlined below. Each code has a sub-code so each transaction will be coded as */***.

Profit/Cost centre	Code	Sub-classification	Sub-code
Sales	10	Power drill sales	PD
		Laser drill sales	LD
Production	20	Direct cost	DC
		Indirect cost	IC
Administration	30	Direct cost	DC
		Indirect cost	IC
Selling and Distribution	40	Direct cost	DC
		Indirect cost	IC

Code the following revenue and expense transactions, which have been extracted from purchase invoices, sales invoices and payroll, using the table below.

Transaction	Code
Rent paid on the workshop	
Electricity for payroll/HR offices	
Sales of laser drills	
Sales of power drills	
Steel for drill heads	
Sales representatives' wages	

Task 1.7

Cockermouth Limited operates a chain of bakeries and uses an alpha-numeric coding system for its elements of cost (materials, labour or overheads) and then further classifies each element by nature (direct or indirect cost) as below. So, for example, the code for direct materials is M100.

Element of cost	Code	Nature of cost	Code
Materials	M	Direct	100
		Indirect	200
Labour	L	Direct	100
		Indirect	200
Overheads	O	Direct	100
		Indirect	200

Code the following costs, extracted from invoices and payroll, using the table below.

Cost	Code
Wages of delivery driver	
Fees for annual audit by local accountants	
Yeast used in baking	
Bakers' salaries	
Wood used to fuel special pizza oven	

Task 1.8

Identify the following statements as either True or False by putting a tick in the relevant column of the table below.

	True	False
Fixed costs are also known as period costs and generally remain the same however many units are produced		
Variable costs change directly with changes in activity		
Employees paid a basic wage plus commission are an example of a semi-variable cost		

Task 1.9

Classify the following costs as either fixed or variable by putting a tick in the relevant column of the table below.

Costs	Fixed	Variable
Chemicals for making paint		
Wages of machine operators paid at a piecework rate		
Salaries of maintenance workers		
Business rates on a car showroom		

Task 1.10

Complete the table below showing fixed costs, variable costs, total costs and unit cost at the different levels of production. The first row has already been completed for you.

Units	Fixed costs	Variable costs	Total costs	Unit cost
500	£20,000	£5,000	£25,000	£50.00
2,500	£	£	£	£
5,000	£	£	£	£
7,500	£	£	£	£

Task 1.11

Maryport Ltd is costing a single product, which has the following cost details:

Variable costs per unit

Materials	£10
Labour	£12
Overheads	£200,000

Complete the following total cost and unit cost table for a production level of 20,000 units.

Element	Total cost	Unit cost
Materials	£	£
Labour	£	£
Overheads	£	£
Total	£	£

Task 1.12

Gretna Ltd makes a single product and for a production level of 10,000 units has the following cost details:

Materials 10,000 kilos at	£10 per kilo
Labour 8,000 hours at	£20 an hour
Overheads	£40,000

Complete the table below to show the unit cost at the production level of 10,000 units.

Element	Unit cost
Materials	£
Labour	£
Overheads	£
Total	£

Section 2

Task 2.1

Reorder the following headings and costs into a manufacturing account format on the right side of the table below for the year ended 30 September.

Heading	£	Manufacturing account	£
MANUFACTURING COST	246,250		
Closing inventory of work in progress	12,500		
Closing inventory of finished goods	31,250		
Opening inventory of raw materials	8,750		
Closing inventory of raw materials	12,500		
DIRECT MATERIALS USED	58,750		
Manufacturing overheads	66,250		
COST OF GOODS SOLD	250,000		
Direct labour	121,250		
COST OF GOODS MANUFACTURED	243,750		
Purchases of raw materials	62,500		
PRIME COST	180,000		
Opening inventory of work in progress	10,000		
Opening inventory of finished goods	37,500		

Task 2.2

Identify the correct inventory valuation method from the characteristic given by putting a tick in the relevant column of the table below.

Characteristic	FIFO	LIFO	AVCO
The first items bought are those issued first			
The most recent purchases are issued first			
Issues are valued at the weighted average cost based on all deliveries to date			

Task 2.3

Identify whether the following statements are True or False by putting a tick in the relevant column of the table below.

	True	False
If costs are increasing FIFO will give a higher inventory valuation than LIFO		
If costs are increasing LIFO will give a higher inventory valuation than FIFO		
AVCO uses the average price to value the next issue or sale		

Task 2.4

Jersey Ltd has the following movements in a certain type of inventory into and out of its stores for the month of July:

DATE	RECEIPTS		ISSUES	
	Units	Cost	Units	Cost
July 5	1,000	£1,500		
July 8	1,500	£3,000		
July 12	2,500	£6,250		
July 20			3,000	
July 25	2,000	£6,000		

Complete the table below for the issue and closing inventory values.

Method	Cost of issue on 20 July	Closing inventory at 31 July
FIFO	£	£
LIFO	£	£
AVCO	£	£

Task 2.5

Identify the following statements as True or False by putting a tick in the relevant column of the table below.

	True	False
The fixed cost per unit rises over the level of output		
Many fixed costs are only fixed over a certain range of output		

Task 2.6

Identify the labour payment method by putting a tick in the relevant column of the table below.

Payment method	Time-rate	Piecework	Piecework plus bonus
This method acts as an incentive to produce more			
A basic amount is paid per hour worked			
If output is better than expected a bonus is paid			

Task 2.7

Identify one advantage for each labour payment method by putting a tick in the relevant column of the table below.

Payment method	Time-rate	Piecework
The quality of the goods produced is not affected by workers rushing a job.		
Fewer inspectors may be needed		
Employee pay remains the same if output fluctuates		

Task 2.8

Exeter Ltd pays a time-rate of £12.50 per hour to its direct labour for a standard 35-hour week. Any of the labour force working in excess of 35 hours is paid an overtime rate of £15 per hour.

Calculate the gross wage for the week for the two workers in the table below.

Worker	Hours worked	Basic wage	Overtime	Gross wage
J Collins	35 hours	£	£	£
M Thatcher	40 hours	£	£	£

Task 2.9

Axminster Ltd uses a piecework method to pay labour in one of its factories. The rate used is 80p per unit produced.

Calculate the gross wage for the week for the two workers in the table below.

Worker	Units produced in week	Gross wage
A Daley	375 units	£
G Cole	435 units	£

Task 2.10

Seaton Ltd uses a time-rate method with bonus to pay its direct labour in one of its factories. The time-rate used is £10.50 per hour and a worker is expected to produce six units an hour, anything over this and the worker is paid a bonus of £1.25 per unit.

Calculate the gross wage for the week including bonus for the three workers in the table below.

Worker	Hours worked	Units produced	Basic wage	Bonus	Gross wage
M Rochester	35	180	£	£	£
J Eyre	35	195	£	£	£
A Grey	35	230	£	£	£

Task 2.11

Identify the following statements as being True or False by putting a tick in the relevant column of the table below.

	True	False
A variance is the difference between budgeted and expected cost		
A favourable variance means actual costs are greater than budgeted costs		

Task 2.12

Colyton Ltd has produced a performance report detailing budgeted and actual cost for last month.

Calculate the amount of the variance for each cost type and then determine whether it is adverse or favourable by typing F for favourable and A for adverse in the right-hand column of the table below.

Cost type	Budget £	Actual £	Variance	Adverse/ Favourable
Direct materials	25,500	20,200	£	
Direct labour	55,000	56,125	£	
Production overheads	35,000	32,120	£	
Administration overheads	15,000	16,950	£	
Selling and Distribution overheads	5,000	4,950	£	

Task 2.13

The following performance report for this month has been produced for Weston Ltd as summarised in the table below. Any variance in excess of 5% of budget is deemed to be significant and should be reported to the relevant manager for review and appropriate action.

Examine the variances in the table below and indicate whether they are significant or not significant by typing S for significant and NS for not significant in the right-hand column below.

Cost type	Budget £	Variance	Adverse/ Favourable	Significant/ Not significant
Direct materials	£170,000	£8,750	Adverse	
Direct labour	£140,000	£9,025	Adverse	
Production overheads	£52,000	£4,218	Favourable	
Administration overheads	£45,000	£5,810	Adverse	
Selling and Distribution overheads	£22,000	£1,500	Adverse	

Task 2.14

It was noted from the performance report for Jedburgh Ltd for an earlier month that the following cost variances were significant:

- Direct labour cost
- Sales overheads

These variances need to be reported to the relevant managers for review and appropriate action if required.

Identify a relevant manager for each significant variance to whom the performance report should be sent.

Variance	Relevant manager
Direct labour cost	▼
Sales overheads	▼

Picklist:

Production manager
Sales manager
HR manager
Administration manager

BPP PRACTICE ASSESSMENT 2
BASIC COSTING

ANSWERS

Basic Costing BPP practice assessment 2

Section 1

Task 1.1

Transaction	Capital	Revenue
Purchase of office furniture for office manager	✓	
Purchase of office furniture by office furniture saleroom for resale		✓
Paying VAT		✓
Making cash sales		✓

Task 1.2

Cost	Materials	Labour	Overheads
Rent and rates on the workshop			✓
Leather for making the boots	✓		
Salary of bookkeeper employed in the business			✓
Wages of two cobblers making lasts for the boots		✓	

Task 1.3

Cost	Direct	Indirect
Supplies of food bought in for the kitchen	✓	
Interest on mortgage to buy the hotel		✓
Hotel cashier's salary		✓
Wages of waiters in the hotel restaurant	✓	

Task 1.4

Cost	Production	Administration	Selling and Distribution
Advertising dinghies in local newspaper			✓
Material for making sails in the factory	✓		
Fees to estate agent for locating new premises		✓	
Salaries of seamstresses stitching material for sails	✓		

Task 1.5

Cost	Fixed	Variable	Semi-variable
Charge for electricity for the kilns firing the pots that includes a standing charge			✓
Annual entertainment budget for the pottery	✓		
Cost of glazes bought in to glaze the pots		✓	
Labour costs for potters paid on a piecework basis		✓	

Task 1.6

Transaction	Code
Rent paid on the workshop	20/IC
Electricity for payroll/HR offices	30/IC
Sales of laser drills	10/LD
Sales of power drills	10/PD
Steel for drill heads	20/DC
Sales representatives' wages	40/DC

Task 1.7

Cost	Code
Wages of delivery driver	L200
Fees for annual audit by local accountants	O200
Yeast used in baking	M100
Bakers' salaries	L100
Wood used to fuel special pizza oven	M200

Task 1.8

	True	False
Fixed costs are also known as period costs and generally remain the same however many units are produced	✓	
Variable costs change directly with changes in activity	✓	
Employees paid a basic wage plus commission are an example of a semi-variable cost	✓	

Task 1.9

Costs	Fixed	Variable
Chemicals for making paint		✓
Wages of machine operators paid at a piecework rate		✓
Salaries of maintenance workers	✓	
Business rates on a car showroom	✓	

Task 1.10

Units	Fixed costs	Variable costs	Total costs	Unit cost
500	£20,000	£5,000	£25,000	£50.00
2,500	£20,000	£25,000	£45,000	£18.00
5,000	£20,000	£50,000	£70,000	£14.00
7,500	£20,000	£75,000	£95,000	£12.67

Task 1.11

Element	Total cost	Unit cost
Materials	£200,000	£10.00
Labour	£240,000	£12.00
Overheads	£200,000	£10.00
Total	£640,000	£32.00

Task 1.12

Element	Unit cost
Materials	£10.00
Labour	£16.00
Overheads	£4.00
Total	£30.00

Section 2

Task 2.1

Manufacturing Account   Y/e 30 September

	£
Opening inventory of raw materials	8,750
Purchases of raw materials	62,500
Closing inventory of raw materials	12,500
DIRECT MATERIALS USED	58,750
Direct labour	121,250
PRIME COST	180,000
Manufacturing overheads	66,250
MANUFACTURING COST	246,250
Opening inventory of work in progress	10,000
Closing inventory of work in progress	12,500
COST OF GOODS MANUFACTURED	243,750
Opening inventory of finished goods	37,500
Closing inventory of finished goods	31,250
COST OF GOODS SOLD	250,000

Task 2.2

Characteristic	FIFO	LIFO	AVCO
The first items bought are those issued first	✓		
The most recent purchases are issued first		✓	
Issues are valued at the weighted average cost based on all deliveries to date			✓

Task 2.3

	True	False
If costs are increasing FIFO will give a higher inventory valuation than LIFO	✓	
If costs are increasing LIFO will give a higher inventory valuation than FIFO		✓
AVCO uses the average price to value the next issue or sale	✓	

Task 2.4

Method	Cost of issue on 20 July	Closing inventory at 31 July
FIFO	£1,500 + £3,000 +(500/2,500 × £6,250) = **£5,750**	£6,000 + (2,000/2,500 × £6,250) = **£11,000**
LIFO	£6,250 + (500/1,500 × £3,000) = **£7,250**	£6,000 + £1,500 + (1,000/1,500 × £3,000) = **£9,500**
AVCO	[(£1,500 + £3,000 + £6,250)/5,000] × 3,000 = **£6,450**	£6,000 + [(£1,500 + £3,000 + £6,250)/5,000 × 2,000] = **£10,300**

Task 2.5

	True	False
The fixed cost per unit rises over the level of output		✓
Many fixed costs are only fixed over a certain range of output	✓	

Task 2.6

Payment method	Time-rate	Piecework	Piecework plus bonus
This method acts as an incentive to produce more		✓	
A basic amount is paid per hour worked	✓		
If output is better than expected a bonus is paid			✓

Task 2.7

Payment method	Time-rate	Piecework
The quality of the goods produced is not affected by workers rushing a job.	✓	
Fewer inspectors may be needed	✓	
Employee pay remains the same if output fluctuates	✓	

Task 2.8

Worker	Hours worked	Basic wage	Overtime	Gross wage
J Collins	35 hours	£437.50	£0.00	£437.50
M Thatcher	40 hours	£437.50	£75.00	£512.50

Task 2.9

Worker	Units produced in week	Gross wage
A Daley	375 units	£300
G Cole	435 units	£348

Task 2.10

Worker	Hours worked	Units produced	Basic wage	Bonus	Gross wage
M Rochester	35	180	£367.50	£0.00	£367.50
J Eyre	35	195	£367.50	£0.00	£367.50
A Grey	35	230	£367.50	£25.00	£392.50

Task 2.11

	True	False
A variance is the difference between budgeted and expected cost		✓
A favourable variance means actual costs are greater than budgeted costs		✓

Task 2.12

Cost type	Variance	Adverse/Favourable
Direct materials	£5,300	F
Direct labour	£1,125	A
Production overheads	£2,880	F
Administration overheads	£1,950	A
Selling and Distribution overheads	£50	F

Task 2.13

Cost type	Significant/Not significant
Direct materials	S
Direct labour	S
Production overheads	S
Administration overheads	S
Selling and Distribution overheads	S

Task 2.14

Variance	Relevant manager
Direct labour cost	Production manager and HR manager
Sales overheads	Sales manager

BPP PRACTICE ASSESSMENT 3
BASIC COSTING

Time allowed: 2 hours

Basic Costing BPP practice assessment 3

Section 1

Task 1.1

A business receives an invoice for a batch order of paint delivered last week.

Indicate which of the characteristics below concern the financial accounting system and which concern the management accounting system by putting a tick in the relevant column of the table below.

Characteristic	Financial accounting	Management accounting
The paint was bought on credit		
The paint was coded to the production cost centre code		
The paint was bought from Albion Paints		

Task 1.2

Asquith Ltd is a manufacturer of gloves.

Classify the following costs by element (materials, labour or overheads) by putting a tick in the relevant column of the table below.

Cost	Materials	Labour	Overheads
Telephone charges for the sales office			
Glue used in making the gloves			
Oil for glove pressing machine			
Salary of the financial controller			

Task 1.3

Baldwin Ltd is in business as sign painters.

Classify the following costs by nature (direct or indirect) by putting a tick in the relevant column of the table below.

Cost	Direct	Indirect
Rent of factory premises		
Varnish used on signboards		
Wages of sign painters		
Wages of supervisor		

Task 1.4

Blair Ltd produces waffle irons.

Classify the following costs by function (production, administration, or finance) by putting a tick in the relevant column of the table below.

Cost	Production	Administration	Finance
Interest on loan taken out to buy new press machines			
Maintenance costs for the press machines			
Wages for part-time secretary to the office manager			
Pig iron used in the waffle moulds to make the waffle irons			

Task 1.5

Brown Ltd is a manufacturer of traditional Scottish fudge.

Classify the following costs by their behaviour (fixed, variable, or semi-variable) by putting a tick in the relevant column of the table below.

Cost	Fixed	Variable	Semi-variable
Packaging for the fudge tablets			
Advertising costs for the year			
Gas for the fudge kettles. This includes a standing charge			
Sugar used to make the fudge			

Task 1.6

Wilson Ltd makes wetsuits. It uses a numerical coding structure based on one profit centre and three cost centres as outlined below. Each code has a sub-code so each transaction will be coded as ***/***.

Profit/Cost centre	Code	Sub-classification	Sub-code
Sales	100	European sales	100
		Asian sales	200
Production	200	Direct cost	100
		Indirect cost	200
Administration	300	Direct cost	100
		Indirect cost	200
Selling and Distribution	400	Direct cost	100
		Indirect cost	200

Code the following revenue and expense transactions, which have been extracted from purchase invoices, sales invoices and payroll, using the table below.

Transaction	Code
Glue used to seal the wetsuits	
Factory rates	
Sales to France	
Sales to China	
Salaries of sales representatives	
Spare parts for stitching machines	

Task 1.7

Heath Limited makes handbags and uses a coding system for its elements of cost (materials, labour or overheads) and then further classifies each element by nature (direct or indirect cost) as below. So, for example, the code for direct materials is M100.

Element of cost	Code	Nature of cost	Code
Materials	M	Direct	100
		Indirect	200
Labour	L	Direct	100
		Indirect	200
Overheads	O	Direct	100
		Indirect	200

Code the following costs, extracted from invoices and payroll, using the table below.

Cost	Code
Salary of bag stitcher	
Monthly fees for bookkeeper to come in and write up the ledgers	
Thread used in stitching bags	
Cleaning materials used to clean the workshop	

Task 1.8

Identify the following statements as either True or False by putting a tick in the relevant column of the table below.

	True	False
Fixed costs are affected in the short term by changes in production level		
Variable costs are also known as period costs		
Cost centres collect together all the costs of an area or department		

Task 1.9

Classify the following costs for a car manufacturer as either fixed or variable by putting a tick in the relevant column of the table below.

Costs	Fixed	Variable
Oil in new cars delivered to showrooms		
Wages of production line workers paid at a time-rate		
Rent of paint shop		
Interest on loan taken out to fund purchase of new robots		

Task 1.10

Complete the table below showing fixed costs, variable costs, total costs and unit cost at the different levels of production.

Units	Fixed costs	Variable costs	Total costs	Unit cost
1,000	£12,000	£6,000	£18,000	£18.00
2,000	£	£	£	£
3,000	£	£	£	£
4,000	£	£	£	£

Task 1.11

Major Ltd is costing a single product, which has the following cost details:

Variable costs per unit

Materials	£7
Labour	£5
Total fixed costs	£50,000

Complete the following total cost and unit cost table for a production level of 10,000 units.

Element	Total cost	Unit cost
Materials	£	£
Labour	£	£
Overheads	£	£
Total	£	£

Task 1.12

Attlee Ltd makes a single product and for a production level of 15,000 units has the following cost details:

Materials 5,000 kilos at	£7 per kilo
Labour 4,000 hours at	£8 an hour
Overheads	£30,000

Complete the table below to show the unit cost at the production level of 15,000 units.

Element	Unit cost
Materials	£
Labour	£
Overheads	£
Total	£

Section 2

Task 2.1

Reorder the following headings and costs into a manufacturing account format on the right side of the table below for the year ended 31 December.

Heading	Cost £	Manufacturing account	£
Closing inventory of work in progress	37,500		
Direct labour	363,750		
Opening inventory of raw materials	26,250		
Closing inventory of finished goods	93,750		
Closing inventory of raw materials	37,500		
Manufacturing overheads	198,750		
COST OF GOODS SOLD	750,000		
MANUFACTURING COST	738,750		
Purchases of raw materials	187,500		
Opening inventory of work in progress	30,000		
Opening inventory of finished goods	112,500		
PRIME COST	540,000		
DIRECT MATERIALS USED	176,250		
COST OF GOODS MANUFACTURED	731,250		

Task 2.2

Identify the correct inventory valuation method from the characteristic given by putting a tick in the relevant column of the table below.

Characteristic	FIFO	LIFO	AVCO
This method would suit businesses with perishable goods where the oldest items are used first			
This method is used where issues are picked from the most recent deliveries at the top of the inventory pile			
This method suits inventories which are mixed when stored eg chemicals			

Task 2.3

Identify whether the following statements are True or False by putting a tick in the relevant column of the table below.

	True	False
LIFO gives the largest inventory valuation when the purchase costs of inventory are rising		
AVCO costs issues of inventory at the oldest purchase price		
FIFO gives the largest inventory valuation when the purchase costs of inventory are rising		

Task 2.4

Walpole Ltd has the following movements in a certain type of inventory into and out of its stores for the month of February:

DATE	RECEIPTS		ISSUES	
	Units	Cost	Units	Cost
February 5	500	£1,000		
February 8	750	£1,875		
February 12	1,250	£2,500		
February 18			1,950	
February 25	1,000	£6,000		

Complete the table below for the issue and closing inventory values.

Method	Cost of issue on 18 February	Closing inventory at 28 February
FIFO	£	£
LIFO	£	£
AVCO	£	£

Task 2.5

Identify the following statements as True or False by putting a tick in the relevant column of the table below.

	True	False
Direct costs are generally variable		
With variable costs, the total cost increases in proportion to the increase in output		

Task 2.6

Identify the labour payment method by putting a tick in the relevant column of the table below.

Payment method	Time-rate	Piecework
An overtime premium is paid for hours above a pre-set maximum		
A differential rate is paid for higher production		
The overtime premium is calculated as the amount paid for an hour's work less the basic rate for that hour		

Task 2.7

Identify each advantage with the appropriate labour payment method by putting a tick in the relevant column of the table below.

Advantage	Time-rate	Piecework
Employees don't rush jobs as they are not paid any more for producing more		
Acts as an incentive for employees to produce more		
More efficient workers are paid more		

Task 2.8

Shaftesbury Ltd pays a time-rate of £5.85 per hour to its direct labour for a standard 35-hour week. Any of the labour force working in excess of 35 hours is paid an overtime rate of £8.20 per hour.

Calculate the gross wage for the week for the two workers in the table below.

Worker	Hours worked	Basic wage	Overtime	Gross wage
G Bundchen	35	£	£	£
L Evangelista	37	£	£	£

Task 2.9

Gladstone Ltd uses a piecework method to pay labour in one of its factories. The rate used is 95p per unit produced.

Calculate the gross wage for the week for the two workers in the table below.

Worker	Units produced in week	Gross wage
M Mouse	550 units	£
W Coyote	490 units	£

Task 2.10

Disraeli Ltd uses a time-rate method with bonus to pay its direct labour in one of its factories. The time-rate used is £13.75 per hour and a worker is expected to produce five units an hour, anything over this and the worker is paid a bonus of £3.50 per unit.

Calculate the gross wage for the week including bonus for the three workers in the table below.

Worker	Hours worked	Units produced	Basic wage	Bonus	Gross wage
D Duck	35	165	£	£	£
F Flintstone	35	173	£	£	£
B Rubble	35	180	£	£	£

Task 2.11

Identify the following statements as being True or False by putting a tick in the relevant column of the table below.

	True	False
A significance report is a formal method of providing information on costs and revenues to management and reporting variances		
Managers are only interested in adverse variances		

Task 2.12

Churchill Ltd has produced a performance report detailing budgeted and actual cost for last month.

Calculate the amount of the variance for each cost type and then determine whether it is adverse or favourable by typing F for favourable and A for adverse in the right-hand column of the table below.

Cost type	Budget £	Actual £	Variance	Adverse/ Favourable
Direct materials	33,750	34,250	£	
Direct labour	35,000	32,125	£	
Production overheads	30,000	29,812	£	
Administration overheads	37,550	38,950	£	
Selling and Distribution overheads	45,000	42,950	£	

Task 2.13

The following performance report for this month has been produced for Macmillan Ltd as summarised in the table below. Any variance in excess of 15% of budget is deemed to be significant and should be reported to the relevant manager for review and appropriate action.

Examine the variances in the table below and indicate whether they are significant or not significant by typing S for significant and NS for not significant in the right-hand column below.

Cost type	Budget	Variance	Adverse/ Favourable	Significant/ Not significant
Direct materials	£122,000	£19,335	Adverse	
Direct labour	£80,000	£8,015	Adverse	
Production overheads	£64,000	£6,208	Favourable	
Administration overheads	£55,000	£14,980	Adverse	
Selling and Distribution overheads	£32,000	£3,150	Adverse	

Task 2.14

It was noted from the performance report for Balfour Ltd for an earlier month that the following cost variances were significant:

- Direct material cost
- Sales overheads

These variances need to be reported to the relevant managers for review and appropriate action, if required.

Identify a relevant manager for each significant variance to whom the performance report should be sent.

Variance	Relevant manager
Direct material cost	▼
Sales overheads	▼

Picklist:

Production manager
Sales manager
HR manager
Administration manager

BPP PRACTICE ASSESSMENT 3
BASIC COSTING

ANSWERS

Basic Costing BPP practice assessment 3

Section 1

Task 1.1

Characteristic	Financial accounting	Management accounting
The paint was bought on credit	✓	
The paint was coded to the production cost centre code		✓
The paint was bought from Albion Paints	✓	

Task 1.2

Cost	Materials	Labour	Overheads
Telephone charges for the sales office			✓
Glue used in making the gloves	✓		
Oil for glove pressing machine			✓
Salary of the financial controller			✓

Task 1.3

Cost	Direct	Indirect
Rent of factory premises		✓
Varnish used on signboards	✓	
Wages of sign painters	✓	
Wages of supervisor		✓

Task 1.4

Cost	Production	Administration	Finance
Interest on loan taken out to buy new press machines			✓
Maintenance costs for the press machines	✓		
Wages for part-time secretary to the office manager		✓	
Pig iron used in the waffle moulds to make the waffle irons	✓		

Task 1.5

Cost	Fixed	Variable	Semi-variable
Packaging for the fudge tablets		✓	
Advertising costs for the year	✓		
Gas for the fudge kettles. This includes a standing charge			✓
Sugar used to make the fudge		✓	

Task 1.6

Transaction	Code
Glue used to seal the wetsuits	200/100
Factory rates	200/200
Sales to France	100/100
Sales to China	100/200
Salaries of sales representatives	400/100
Spare parts for stitching machines	200/200

Task 1.7

Cost	Code
Salary of bag stitcher	L100
Monthly fees for bookkeeper to come in and write up the ledgers	O200
Thread used in stitching bags	M100
Cleaning materials used to clean the workshop	M200

Task 1.8

	True	False
Fixed costs are affected in the short term by changes in production level		✓
Variable costs are also known as period costs		✓
Cost centres collect together all the costs of an area or department	✓	

Task 1.9

Costs	Fixed	Variable
Oil in new cars delivered to showrooms		✓
Wages of production line workers paid at a time-rate	✓	
Rent of paint shop	✓	
Interest on loan taken out to fund purchase of new robots	✓	

Task 1.10

Units	Fixed costs	Variable costs	Total costs	Unit cost
1,000	£12,000	£6,000	£18,000	£18.00
2,000	£12,000	£12,000	£24,000	£12.00
3,000	£12,000	£18,000	£30,000	£10.00
4,000	£12,000	£24,000	£36,000	£9.00

Task 1.11

Element	Total cost	Unit cost
Materials	£70,000	£7.00
Labour	£50,000	£5.00
Overheads	£50,000	£5.00
Total	£170,000	£17.00

Task 1.12

Element	Unit cost
Materials	£2.33
Labour	£2.13
Overheads	£2.00
Total	£6.46

Section 2

Task 2.1

Manufacturing Account   Y/e 31 December

	£
Opening inventory of raw materials	26,250
Purchases of raw materials	187,500
Closing inventory of raw materials	37,500
DIRECT MATERIALS USED	176,250
Direct labour	363,750
PRIME COST	540,000
Manufacturing overheads	198,750
MANUFACTURING COST	738,750
Opening inventory of work in progress	30,000
Closing inventory of work in progress	37,500
COST OF GOODS MANUFACTURED	731,250
Opening inventory of finished goods	112,500
Closing inventory of finished goods	93,750
COST OF GOODS SOLD	750,000

Task 2.2

Characteristic	FIFO	LIFO	AVCO
This method would suit businesses with perishable goods where the oldest items are used first	✓		
This method is used where issues are picked from the most recent deliveries at the top of the inventory pile		✓	
This method suits inventories which are mixed when stored eg chemicals			✓

Task 2.3

	True	False
LIFO gives the largest inventory valuation when the purchase costs of inventory are rising		✓
AVCO costs issues of inventory at the oldest purchase price		✓
FIFO gives the largest inventory valuation when the purchase costs of inventory are rising	✓	

Task 2.4

Method	Cost of issue on 18 February	Closing inventory at 28 February
FIFO	(1,000 + 1,875 + (700/1,250 × 2,500)) = **£4,275**	6,000 + (550/1,250 × 2,500) = **£7,100**
LIFO	(2,500 + (700/750 × 1,875)) = **£4,250**	(6,000 + 1,000 + (50/750 × 1,875)) = **£7,125**
AVCO	1,950/2,500 × 5,375 = **£4,192.50**	(550/2,500 × 5,375) + 6,000 = **£7,182.50**

Task 2.5

	True	False
Direct costs are generally variable	✓	
With variable costs, the total cost increases in proportion to the increase in output	✓	

Task 2.6

Payment method	Time-rate	Piecework
An overtime premium is paid for hours above a pre-set maximum	✓	
A differential rate is paid for higher production		✓
The overtime premium is calculated as the amount paid for an hour's work less the basic rate for that hour	✓	

Task 2.7

Advantage	Time-rate	Piecework
Employees don't rush jobs as they are not paid any more for producing more	✓	
Acts as an incentive for employees to produce more		✓
More efficient workers are paid more		✓

Task 2.8

Worker	Hours worked	Basic wage	Overtime	Gross wage
G Bundchen	35	£204.75	£0.00	£204.75
L Evangelista	37	£204.75	£16.40	£221.15

Task 2.9

Worker	Units produced in week	Gross wage
M Mouse	550 units	£522.50
W Coyote	490 units	£465.50

Task 2.10

Worker	Hours worked	Units produced	Basic wage	Bonus	Gross wage
D Duck	35	165	£481.25	£0.00	£481.25
F Flintstone	35	173	£481.25	£0.00	£481.25
B Rubble	35	180	£481.25	£17.50	£498.75

Task 2.11

	True	False
A significance report is a formal method of providing information on costs and revenues to management and reporting variances	✓	
Managers are only interested in adverse variances		✓

Task 2.12

Cost type	Budget £	Actual £	Variance	Adverse/ Favourable
Direct materials	33,750	34,250	£500	A
Direct labour	35,000	32,125	£2,875	F
Production overheads	30,000	29,812	£188	F
Administration overheads	37,550	38,950	£1,400	A
Selling and Distribution overheads	45,000	42,950	£2,050	F

Task 2.13

Cost type	Budget	Variance	Adverse/ Favourable	Significant/ Not significant
Direct materials	£122,000	£19,335	Adverse	S
Direct labour	£80,000	£8,015	Adverse	NS
Production overheads	£64,000	£6,208	Favourable	NS
Administration overheads	£55,000	£14,980	Adverse	S
Selling and Distribution overheads	£32,000	£3,150	Adverse	NS

Task 2.14

Variance	Relevant manager
Direct material cost	Production manager
Sales overheads	Sales manager

BPP PRACTICE ASSESSMENT 4
BASIC COSTING

Time allowed: 2 hours

Basic Costing BPP practice assessment 4

Section 1

Task 1.1

Management are constantly making decisions about how the business operates. These are short-term, medium-term or long-term decisions. The table below lists an example of each type.

Match the example to the correct decision by putting a tick in the relevant column of the table below.

Characteristic	Short-term	Medium-term	Long-term
Where to locate a factory			
Whether to work overtime in the factory			
Whether to take out a further loan to finance the business			

Task 1.2

Clifton Ltd makes glass bottles.

Classify the following costs by element (materials, labour or overheads) by putting a tick in the relevant column of the table below.

Cost	Materials	Labour	Overheads
Spare parts for the glass firing kiln			
Rent on the workshop			
Salaries of glass blowers			
Sand used in making the bottles			

Task 1.3

Easton Ltd operates as a petrol station.

Classify the following costs by nature (direct or indirect) by putting a tick in the relevant column of the table below.

Cost	Direct	Indirect
Petrol in the pumps		
Business rates for the petrol station		
Wages of pump attendants		
Salary of forecourt supervisor for the petrol company		

Task 1.4

St Paul Ltd makes guitars.

Classify the following costs by function (production, administration, or selling and distribution) by putting a tick in the relevant column of the table below.

Cost	Production	Administration	Selling and Distribution
Purchase of balsa wood for making guitars			
Advertising the instruments in *Music Weekly*			
Secretarial wages			
Salaries of craftspeople making the instruments			

Task 1.5

Highbridge Ltd is a manufacturer of children's toys.

Classify the following costs by their behaviour (fixed, variable, or semi-variable) by putting a tick in the relevant column of the table below.

Cost	Fixed	Variable	Semi-variable
Felt used in making the toys			
Marketing costs for the year			
Telephone charges for the office that include a fixed line rental and call charges			
Electricity charges for the sewing machines that include a basic charge and a unit consumption charge			

Task 1.6

Burnham Ltd makes bicycles. It uses a numerical coding structure based on one profit centre and three cost centres as outlined below. Each code has a sub-code so each transaction will be coded as */***.

Profit/Cost centre	Code	Sub-classification	Sub-code
Sales	9	Children's bike sales	100
		Adult bike sales	200
Production	8	Direct cost	100
		Indirect cost	200
Administration	7	Direct cost	100
		Indirect cost	200
Selling and Distribution	6	Direct cost	100
		Indirect cost	200

Code the following revenue and expense transactions, which have been extracted from purchase invoices, sales invoices and payroll, using the table below.

Transaction	Code
Electricity charge for the upstairs offices	
Petrol for warehouse van	
Sales of adult bikes	
Sales of children's bikes	
Enamel paint for bicycles	
Factory supervisor wages	

Task 1.7

Weston Limited operates a convenience store and uses a coding system for its elements of cost (materials, labour or overheads) and then further classifies each element by nature (direct or indirect cost) as below. So, for example, the code for direct materials is M100.

Element of cost	Code	Nature of cost	Code
Materials	M	Direct	100
		Indirect	200
Labour	L	Direct	100
		Indirect	200
Overheads	O	Direct	100
		Indirect	200

Code the following costs, extracted from invoices and payroll, using the table below.

Cost	Code
Wages of shop staff	
Fees for bookkeeper	
Wholesale cost of newspapers	
Cleaning materials used by shop cleaner	
Rent and rates on the shop premises	

Task 1.8

Identify the following statements as either True or False by putting a tick in the relevant column of the table below.

	True	False
Fixed costs are not affected in the short term by changes in production level		
Variable costs are often known as period costs		
Semi-variable costs are fixed over a certain range of activity		

Task 1.9

Classify the following costs for a boat manufacturer as either fixed or variable by putting a tick in the relevant column of the table below.

Costs	Fixed	Variable
Steel used in making boat hull		
Wages of workers on the assembly line paid piece-rate		
Salaries of managers		
Rent for offices used by sales staff		

Task 1.10

Complete the table below showing fixed costs, variable costs, total costs and unit cost at the different levels of production.

Units	Fixed costs	Variable costs	Total costs	Unit cost
1,000	£25,000	£15,000	£40,000	£40.00
2,000				
3,000				
4,000				

Task 1.11

Taunton Ltd is costing a single product, which has the following cost details:

Variable costs per unit

Materials	£6.50
Labour	£8.50
Total fixed costs	£150,000

Complete the following total cost and unit cost table for a production level of 10,000 units.

Element	Total cost	Unit cost
Materials		
Labour		
Overheads		
Total		

Task 1.12

Kingswear Ltd makes a single product and for a production level of 30,000 units has the following cost details:

Materials 6,000 kilos at	£15 per kilo
Labour 5,000 hours at	£12 an hour
Overheads	£50,000

Complete the table below to show the unit cost at the production level of 30,000 units.

Element	Unit cost
Materials	
Labour	
Overheads	
Total	

Section 2

Task 2.1

Reorder the following headings and costs into a manufacturing account format on the right side of the table below for the year ended 31 January.

Heading	Cost £	Manufacturing account	£
Closing inventory of work in progress	27,150		
Direct labour	244,150		
Opening inventory of raw materials	19,150		
Closing inventory of finished goods	64,150		
Closing inventory of raw materials	27,150		
Manufacturing overheads	134,150		
COST OF GOODS SOLD	505,450		
MANUFACTURING COST	497,450		
Purchases of raw materials	127,150		
Opening inventory of work in progress	22,150		
Opening inventory of finished goods	77,150		
PRIME COST	363,300		
DIRECT MATERIALS USED	119,150		
COST OF GOODS MANUFACTURED	492,450		

Task 2.2

Identify the correct type of inventory from the description given by putting a tick in the relevant column of the table below.

Characteristic	Raw materials	Work in progress	Finished goods
Inventory is kept until ready to be transferred to the production line			
Inventory can be kept for several years for instance whisky manufacturers will keep whisky as it matures			
Inventory is kept so that the demand from customers may be met			

Task 2.3

Identify whether the following statements are True or False by putting a tick in the relevant column of the table below.

	True	False
FIFO assumes the first items bought will be the first items issued.		
AVCO recalculates the cost of inventory each time an issue is made		
LIFO costs issues of inventory at the latest prices		
FIFO values closing inventory at the earliest purchase price		
LIFO values closing inventory at the earliest purchase price		
AVCO is most suitable where inventorys are mixed together for instance chemicals		

Task 2.4

Wellington Ltd has the following movements in a certain type of inventory into and out of its stores for the month of April:

DATE	RECEIPTS		ISSUES	
	Units	Cost	Units	Cost
April 10	300	£1,200		
April 11	450	£2,250		
April 12	1,250	£6,250		
April 19			1,500	
April 27	700	£4,900		

Complete the table below for the issue and closing inventory values.

Method	Cost of issue on 19 April	Closing inventory at 30 April
FIFO		
LIFO		
AVCO		

- -

Task 2.5

Identify the following statements as True or False by putting a tick in the relevant column of the table below.

	True	False
Variable cost per unit remains constant over the level of activity		
Overheads always remain constant over any range of activity		

- -

Task 2.6

Identify the description of the labour payment method by putting a tick in the relevant column of the table below.

Description	Time-rate	Piecework	Differential piecework
Pay is based on units completed by a particular employee			
Pay is based on hours worked and pay per hour			
If production exceeds a certain level higher amounts are paid			

Task 2.7

Identify one advantage for each labour payment method by putting a tick in the relevant column of the table below.

Advantage	Time-rate	Piecework
Quality is a priority as pay is the same no matter how much is produced		
This method gives employees an incentive to produce more		
Can be used for all direct labour employees		

Task 2.8

Park Street Ltd pays a time-rate of £9.75 per hour to its direct labour for a standard 35-hour week. Any of the labour force working in excess of 35 hours is paid an overtime rate of £12.50 per hour.

Calculate the gross wage for the week for the two workers in the table below.

Worker	Hours worked	Basic wage	Overtime	Gross wage
L Hornby	35 hours			
J Shrimpton	42 hours			

Task 2.9

Burnham Ltd uses a piecework method to pay labour in one of its factories. The rate used is 75p per unit produced.

Calculate the gross wage for the week for the two workers in the table below.

Worker	Units produced in week	Gross wage
N Campbell	375 units	
K Moss	390 units	

Task 2.10

Bristol Ltd uses a time-rate method with bonus to pay its direct labour in one of its factories. The time-rate used is £10.50 per hour and a worker is expected to produce six units an hour, anything over this and the worker is paid a bonus of £1.50 per unit.

Calculate the gross wage for the week including bonus for the three workers in the table below.

Worker	Hours worked	Units produced	Basic wage	Bonus	Gross wage
A Einstein	35	160			
N Bohr	35	175			
E Fermi	35	220			

Task 2.11

Identify the following statements as being True or False by putting a tick in the relevant column of the table below.

	True	False
An adverse variance means actual costs are greater than budgeted costs		
A favourable variance means budgeted sales are greater than actual sales		

Task 2.12

Wills Ltd has produced a performance report detailing budgeted and actual cost for last month.

Calculate the amount of the variance for each cost type and then determine whether it is adverse or favourable by typing F for favourable and A for adverse in the right-hand column of the table below.

Cost type	Budget £	Actual £	Variance	Adverse/Favourable
Direct materials	25,500	26,200		
Direct labour	57,000	73,125		
Production overheads	18,000	15,120		
Administration overheads	22,000	21,950		
Selling and Distribution overheads	23,000	24,950		

Task 2.13

The following performance report for this month has been produced for Tiverton Ltd as summarised in the table below. Any variance in excess of 10% of budget is deemed to be significant and should be reported to the relevant manager for review and appropriate action.

Examine the variances in the table below and indicate whether they are significant or not significant by typing S for significant and NS for not significant in the right-hand column below.

Cost type	Budget	Variance	Adverse/ Favourable	Significant/ Not significant
Direct materials	£125,000	£12,335	Favourable	
Direct labour	£20,000	£4,010	Adverse	
Production overheads	£45,000	£4,208	Favourable	
Administration overheads	£34,000	£980	Adverse	
Selling and Distribution overheads	£25,000	£3,120	Favourable	

Task 2.14

It was noted from the performance report for Dawlish Ltd for an earlier month that the following cost variances were significant:

- Direct labour cost
- Administration overheads

These variances needed to be reported to the relevant managers for review and appropriate action if required.

Identify from the list below a relevant manager for each significant variance to whom the performance report should be sent and type the correct entry next to the variance.

Variance	Relevant manager
Direct labour cost	▼
Administration overheads	▼

Picklist:

Production manager
Sales manager
HR manager
Administration manager

BPP PRACTICE ASSESSMENT 4
BASIC COSTING

ANSWERS

Basic Costing BPP practice assessment 4

Section 1

Task 1.1

Characteristic	Short-term	Medium-term	Long-term
Where to locate a factory			✓
Whether to work overtime in the factory	✓		
Whether to take out a further loan to finance the business		✓	

Task 1.2

Cost	Materials	Labour	Overheads
Spare parts for the glass firing kiln	✓		
Rent on the workshop			✓
Salaries of glass blowers		✓	
Sand used in making the bottles	✓		

Task 1.3

Cost	Direct	Indirect
Petrol in the pumps	✓	
Business rates for the petrol station		✓
Wages of pump attendants	✓	
Salary of forecourt supervisor for the petrol company		✓

Task 1.4

Cost	Production	Administration	Selling and Distribution
Purchase of balsa wood for making guitars	✓		
Advertising the instruments in *Music Weekly*			✓
Secretarial wages		✓	
Salaries of craftspeople making the instruments	✓		

Task 1.5

Cost	Fixed	Variable	Semi-variable
Felt used in making the toys		✓	
Marketing costs for the year	✓		
Telephone charges for the office that include a fixed line rental and call charges			✓
Electricity charges for the sewing machines that include a basic charge and a unit consumption charge			✓

Task 1.6

Transaction	Code
Electricity charge for the upstairs offices	7/200
Petrol for warehouse van	6/100
Sales of adult bikes	9/200
Sales of children's bikes	9/100
Enamel paint for bicycles	8/100
Factory supervisor wages	8/200

Task 1.7

Cost	Code
Wages of shop staff	L100
Fees for bookkeeper	O200
Wholesale cost of newspapers	M100
Cleaning materials used by shop cleaner	M200
Rent and rates on the shop premises	O200

Task 1.8

	True	False
Fixed costs are not affected in the short term by changes in production level	✓	
Variable costs are often known as period costs		✓
Semi-variable costs are fixed over a certain range of activity		✓

Task 1.9

Costs	Fixed	Variable
Steel used in making boat hull		✓
Wages of workers on the assembly line paid piece-rate		✓
Salaries of managers	✓	
Rent for offices used by sales staff	✓	

Task 1.10

Units	Fixed costs	Variable costs	Total costs	Unit cost
1,000	£25,000	£15,000	£40,000	£40.00
2,000	£25,000	£30,000	£55,000	£27.50
3,000	£25,000	£45,000	£70,000	£23.33
4,000	£25,000	£60,000	£85,000	£21.25

Task 1.11

Element	Total cost	Unit cost
Materials	£65,000	£6.50
Labour	£85,000	£8.50
Overheads	£150,000	£15.00
Total	£300,000	£30.00

Task 1.12

Element	Unit cost
Materials	£3.00
Labour	£2.00
Overheads	£1.67
Total	£6.67

Section 2

Task 2.1

Manufacturing Account   Y/e 31 January

	£
Opening inventory of raw materials	19,150
Purchases of raw materials	127,150
Closing inventory of raw materials	27,150
DIRECT MATERIALS USED	119,150
Direct labour	244,150
PRIME COST	363,300
Manufacturing overheads	134,150
MANUFACTURING COST	497,450
Opening inventory of work in progress	22,150
Closing inventory of work in progress	27,150
COST OF GOODS MANUFACTURED	492,450
Opening inventory of finished goods	77,150
Closing inventory of finished goods	64,150
COST OF GOODS SOLD	505,450

Task 2.2

Characteristic	Raw materials	Work in progress	Finished goods
Inventory is kept until ready to be transferred to the production line	✓		
Inventory can be kept for several years for instance whisky manufacturers will keep whisky as it matures		✓	
Inventory is kept so that the demand from customers may be met			✓

Task 2.3

	True	False
FIFO assumes the first items bought will be the first items issued.	✓	
AVCO recalculates the cost of inventory each time an issue is made		✓
LIFO costs issues of inventory at the latest prices	✓	
FIFO values closing inventory at the earliest purchase price		✓
LIFO values closing inventory at the earliest purchase price	✓	
AVCO is most suitable where inventories are mixed together for instance chemicals	✓	

Task 2.4

Method	Cost of issue on 19 April	Closing inventory at 30 April
FIFO	(1,200 + 2,250 + (750/1,250 × 6,250)) = **£7,200**	(4,900 + (500/1,250 × 6,250)) = **£7,400**
LIFO	(6,250 + (250/450 × 2,250)) = **£7,500**	(4,900 + 1,200 + (200/450 × 2,250)) = **£7,100**
AVCO	1,500/2,000 × 9,700 = **£7,275**	(4,900 + (500/2,000 × 9,700)) = **£7,325**

Task 2.5

	True	False
Variable cost per unit remains constant over the level of activity	✓	
Overheads always remain constant over any range of activity		✓

Task 2.6

Description	Time-rate	Piecework	Differential piecework
Pay is based on units completed by a particular employee		✓	
Pay is based on hours worked and pay per hour	✓		
If production exceeds a certain level higher amounts are paid			✓

Task 2.7

Advantage	Time-rate	Piecework
Quality is a priority as pay is the same no matter how much is produced	✓	
This method gives employees an incentive to produce more		✓
Can be used for all direct labour employees	✓	

Task 2.8

Worker	Hours worked	Basic wage	Overtime	Gross wage
L Hornby	35 hours	£341.25	£0.00	£341.25
J Shrimpton	42 hours	£341.25	£87.50	£428.75

Task 2.9

Worker	Units produced in week	Gross wage
N Campbell	375 units	£281.25
K Moss	390 units	£292.50

Task 2.10

Worker	Hours worked	Units produced	Basic wage	Bonus	Gross wage
A Einstein	35	160	£367.50	£0	£367.50
N Bohr	35	175	£367.50	£0	£367.50
E Fermi	35	220	£367.50	£15	£382.50

Task 2.11

	True	False
An adverse variance means actual costs are greater than budgeted costs	✓	
A favourable variance means budgeted sales are greater than actual sales		✓

Task 2.12

Cost type	Budget £	Actual £	Variance	Adverse/ Favourable
Direct materials	25,500	26,200	£700	A
Direct labour	57,000	73,125	£16,125	A
Production overheads	18,000	15,120	£2,880	F
Administration overheads	22,000	21,950	£50	F
Selling and Distribution overheads	23,000	24,950	£1,950	A

Task 2.13

Cost type	Budget	Variance	Adverse/ Favourable	Significant/ Not significant
Direct materials	£125,000	£12,335	Favourable	NS
Direct labour	£20,000	£4,010	Adverse	S
Production overheads	£45,000	£4,208	Favourable	NS
Administration overheads	£34,000	£980	Adverse	NS
Selling and Distribution overheads	£25,000	£3,120	Favourable	S

Task 2.14

Variance	Relevant manager
Direct labour cost	Production manager OR HR manager
Administration overheads	Administration manager

BPP PRACTICE ASSESSMENT 5
BASIC COSTING

Time allowed: 2 hours

PRACTICE ASSESSMENT 5

Basic Costing BPP practice assessment 5

Section 1

Task 1.1

There are three main types of business covered in the Basic Costing unit.

Look at the descriptions in the table below and match them to the type of business.

Description	Sole trader	Partnership	Limited company
A group of individuals who trade together intending to make a profit			
Shareholders own the business but it is managed by directors and managers			
The owner trades under their own name			

Task 1.2

Hayes Ltd makes wind chimes.

Classify the following costs by element (materials, labour or overheads) by putting a tick in the relevant column of the table below.

Cost	Materials	Labour	Overheads
Wages of machine operators making the chimes			
Telephone charges for workshop floor telephone			
Tin used in making the chimes			
Salary of the supervisor on the workshop floor			

Task 1.3

Elmer Ltd is in business as a tailor of men's clothing.

Classify the following costs by nature (direct or indirect) by putting a tick in the relevant column of the table below.

Cost	Direct	Indirect
Buttons used on suit jackets		
Rent and rates for shop and workshop		
Licences paid to designers each time a suit pattern is used		
Oil for sewing machines		

Task 1.4

Clockhouse Ltd makes clocks.

Classify the following costs by function (production, administration, or financing) by putting a tick in the relevant column of the table below.

Cost	Production	Administration	Financing
Cogs used in timing movements			
Wages of payroll staff			
Overdraft charges			
Salaries of clockmakers			

Task 1.5

West Wickham Ltd is a manufacturer of fibreglass panels.

Classify the following costs by their behaviour (fixed, variable, or semi-variable) by putting a tick in the relevant column of the table below.

Cost	Fixed	Variable	Semi-variable
Spun fibre used in making the panels			
Salary of supervisor on the factory floor			
Electricity costs for the machines that include a standing charge			
Labour costs paid on a piecework basis			

Task 1.6

Catford Ltd makes toys for cats. It uses a alpha-numerical coding structure based on one profit centre and three cost centres as outlined below. Each code has a sub-code so each transaction will be coded as */***.

Profit/Cost centre	Code	Sub-classification	Sub-code
Sales	A	UK sales	100
		Overseas sales	200
Production	B	Direct cost	100
		Indirect cost	200
Administration	C	Direct cost	100
		Indirect cost	200
Selling and Distribution	D	Direct cost	100
		Indirect cost	200

Code the following revenue and expense transactions, which have been extracted from purchase invoices, sales invoices and payroll, using the table below.

Transaction	Code
Telephone charges for the payroll department	
Factory rates	
Sales to Japan	
Sales to Greater Manchester	
Material for toys	
Petrol for sales vans	

Task 1.7

Ladywell Limited operates a day spa and uses a coding system for its elements of cost (materials, labour or overheads) and then further classifies each element by nature (direct or indirect cost) as below. So, for example, the code for direct materials is A100.

Element of cost	Code	Nature of cost	Code
Materials	A	Direct	100
		Indirect	200
Labour	B	Direct	100
		Indirect	200
Overheads	C	Direct	100
		Indirect	200

Code the following costs, extracted from invoices and payroll, using the table below.

Cost	Code
Wages of spa therapists	
Fees for designer creating new website for spa	
Spa salts and minerals used in treatments	
Cleaning materials used by cleaners at the spa	
Maintenance staff wages	

Task 1.8

Identify the following statements as either True or False by putting a tick in the relevant column of the table below.

	True	False
Fixed costs remain the same at different output levels		
Many fixed costs are only fixed over a certain range of output		
A fixed cost per unit decreases as output increases		

Task 1.9

Classify the following costs as either fixed or variable by putting a tick in the relevant column of the table below.

Costs	Fixed	Variable
Cost of ink used in a printing press		
Straightline depreciation on plant and machinery		
Salary of supervisor		
Timber for making chairs in furniture factory		

Task 1.10

Complete the table below showing fixed costs, variable costs, total costs and unit cost at the different levels of production

Units	Fixed costs	Variable costs	Total costs	Unit cost
1,000	£10,000	£8,250	£18,250	£18.25
2,000				
3,000				
4,000				

Task 1.11

Lewisham Ltd is costing a single product, which has the following cost details:

Variable costs per unit

Materials	£7.50
Labour	£5.50
Total fixed costs	£130,000

Complete the following total cost and unit cost table for a production level of 13,000 units.

Element	Total cost	Unit cost
Materials		
Labour		
Overheads		
Total		

Task 1.12

Christobel Ltd makes a single product and for a production level of 150,000 units has the following cost details:

Materials 15,000 kilos at	£10 per kilo
Labour 7,500 hours at	£15 an hour
Overheads	£30,000

Complete the table below to show the unit cost at the production level of 150,000 units.

Element	Unit cost
Materials	
Labour	
Overheads	
Total	

Section 2

Task 2.1

Reorder the following headings and costs into a manufacturing account format on the right side of the table below for the year ended 31 December.

Heading	Cost £	Manufacturing costs	£
Closing inventory of work in progress	35,000		
Direct labour	252,500		
Opening inventory of raw materials	27,500		
Closing inventory of finished goods	72,500		
Closing inventory of raw materials	35,000		
Manufacturing overheads	142,500		
COST OF GOODS SOLD	530,000		
MANUFACTURING COST	522,500		
Purchases of raw materials	135,000		
Opening inventory of work in progress	30,000		
Opening inventory of finished goods	85,000		
PRIME COST	380,000		
DIRECT MATERIALS USED	127,500		
COST OF GOODS MANUFACTURED	517,500		

Task 2.2

Identify the correct inventory valuation method from the characteristic given by putting a tick in the relevant column of the table below.

Characteristic	FIFO	LIFO	AVCO
The earliest invoice prices are used up first, working forward through to the latest prices			
The most recent purchases are issued first			
The best method if inventories are mixed when they are stored			

Task 2.3

Identify whether the following statements are True or False by putting a tick in the relevant column of the table below.

	True	False
LIFO costs issues of inventory at the oldest purchase price		
AVCO costs issues of inventory at the oldest purchase price		
FIFO costs issues of inventory at the oldest purchase price		
LIFO values closing inventory at the most recent purchase price		
FIFO values closing inventory at the most recent purchase price		
AVCO values closing inventory at the latest purchase price		

Task 2.4

New Cross Ltd has the following movements in a certain type of inventory into and out of its stores for the month of August:

DATE	RECEIPTS		ISSUES	
	Units	Cost	Units	Cost
August 5	300	£1,500		
August 8	800	£4,000		
August 12	1,250	£7,500		
August 18			2,100	
August 25	1,000	£6,000		

Complete the table below for the issue and closing inventory values.

Method	Cost of issue on 18 August	Closing inventory at 31 August
FIFO		
LIFO		
AVCO		

- -

Task 2.5

Identify the following statements as True or False by putting a tick in the relevant column of the table below.

	True	False
The fixed cost per unit rises over the level of output		
The variable cost per unit remains constant over the level of output		

- -

Task 2.6

From the characteristics listed, identify the labour payment method by putting a tick in the relevant column of the table below.

Characteristic	Time-rate	Piecework	Time-rate with overtime
Payment is made for each unit or task successfully completed			
Workers are paid a day rate based on the hours they work			
Overtime is paid for hours in excess of the basic agreed level			

Task 2.7

Identify one advantage for each labour payment method by putting a tick in the relevant column of the table below.

Advantage	Time-rate	Piecework
Production problems won't lead to a cut in pay		
Provides incentives to produce more		
Quality less of a priority with this method		

Task 2.8

Charing Cross Ltd pays a time-rate of £14 per hour to its direct labour for a standard 35-hour week. Any of the labour force working in excess of 35 hours is paid an overtime rate of £28 per hour.

Calculate the gross wage for the week for the two workers in the table below.

Worker	Hours worked	Basic wage	Overtime	Gross wage
S Toni	35			
A Partridge	39			

Task 2.9

London Bridge Ltd uses a piecework method to pay labour in one of its factories. The rate used is 65p per unit produced.

Calculate the gross wage for the week for the two workers in the table below.

Worker	Units produced in week	Gross wage
C Hynde	450	
D Harry	390	

Task 2.10

Waterloo Ltd uses a time-rate method with bonus to pay its direct labour in one of its factories. The time-rate used is £11.50 per hour and a worker is expected to produce 4 units an hour, anything over this and the worker is paid a bonus of £1.50 per unit.

Calculate the gross wage for the week including bonus for the three workers in the table below.

Worker	Hours worked	Units produced	Basic wage	Bonus	Gross wage
M Jagger	35	130			
K Richard	35	139			
C Watts	35	160			

Task 2.11

Identify the following statements as being True or False by putting a tick in the relevant column of the table below.

	True	False
Variances only measure the difference between budgeted and actual cost and not budgeted and actual income		
An unfavourable variance means budgeted costs are greater than actual costs		

Task 2.12

Croydon Ltd has produced a performance report detailing budgeted and actual cost for last month.

Calculate the amount of the variance for each cost type and then determine whether it is adverse or favourable by typing F for favourable and A for adverse in the right-hand column of the table below.

Cost type	Budget £	Actual £	Variance	Adverse/Favourable
Direct materials	14,500	12,200		
Direct labour	5,000	3,125		
Production overheads	4,000	6,120		
Administration overheads	3,000	4,950		
Selling and Distribution overheads	5,000	2,950		

Task 2.13

The following performance report for this month has been produced for Selworthy Ltd as summarised in the table below. Any variance in excess of 10% of budget is deemed to be significant and should be reported to the relevant manager for review and appropriate action.

Examine the variances in the table below and indicate whether they are significant or not significant by typing S for significant and NS for not significant in the right-hand column below.

Cost type	Budget	Variance	Adverse/ Favourable	Significant/ Not significant
Direct materials	£5,000	£335	Adverse	
Direct labour	£7,000	£815	Adverse	
Production overheads	£6,000	£428	Favourable	
Administration overheads	£4,000	£580	Adverse	
Selling and Distribution overheads	£2,000	£150	Adverse	

Task 2.14

It was noted from the performance report for Three Bridges Ltd for an earlier month that the following cost variances were significant:

- Direct material cost
- Advertising and Sales overheads

These variances needed to be reported to the relevant managers for review and appropriate action if required.

Identify a relevant manager for each significant variance to whom the performance report should be sent.

Variance	Relevant manager
Direct material cost	▼
Advertising and sales overheads	▼

Picklist:

Production manager
Sales manager
HR manager
Administration manager

BPP PRACTICE ASSESSMENT 5
BASIC COSTING

ANSWERS

Basic Costing BPP practice assessment 5

Section 1

Task 1.1

Description	Sole trader	Partnership	Limited company
A group of individuals who trade together intending to make a profit		✓	
Shareholders own the business but it is managed by directors and managers			✓
The owner trades under their own name	✓		

Task 1.2

Cost	Materials	Labour	Overheads
Wages of machine operators making the chimes		✓	
Telephone charges for workshop floor telephone			✓
Tin used in making the chimes	✓		
Salary of the supervisor on the workshop floor			✓

Task 1.3

Cost	Direct	Indirect
Buttons used on suit jackets	✓	
Rent and rates for shop and workshop		✓
Licences paid to designers each time a suit pattern is used	✓	
Oil for sewing machines		✓

Task 1.4

Cost	Production	Administration	Financing
Cogs used in timing movements	✓		
Wages of payroll staff		✓	
Overdraft charges			✓
Salaries of clockmakers	✓		

Task 1.5

Cost	Fixed	Variable	Semi-variable
Spun fibre used in making the panels		✓	
Salary of supervisor on the factory floor	✓		
Electricity costs for the machines that include a standing charge			✓
Labour costs paid on a piecework basis		✓	

Task 1.6

Transaction	Code
Telephone charges for the payroll department	C/200
Factory rates	B/200
Sales to Japan	A/200
Sales to Greater Manchester	A/100
Material for toys	B/100
Petrol for sales vans	D/100

Task 1.7

Cost	Code
Wages of spa therapists	B100
Fees for designer creating new website for spa	C200
Spa salts and minerals used in treatments	A100
Cleaning materials used by cleaners at the spa	A200
Maintenance staff wages	B200

Task 1.8

	True	False
Fixed costs remain the same at different output levels	✓	
Many fixed costs are only fixed over a certain range of output	✓	
The fixed cost per unit decreases as output increases	✓	

Task 1.9

Costs	Fixed	Variable
Cost of ink used in a printing press		✓
Straightline depreciation on plant and machinery	✓	
Salary of supervisor	✓	
Timber for making chairs in furniture factory		✓

Task 1.10

Units	Fixed costs	Variable costs	Total costs	Unit cost
1,000	£10,000	£8,250	£18,250	£18.25
2,000	£10,000	£16,500	£26,500	£13.25
3,000	£10,000	£24,750	£34,750	£11.58
4,000	£10,000	£33,000	£43,000	£10.75

Task 1.11

Element	Total cost	Unit cost
Materials	£97,500	£7.50
Labour	£71,500	£5.50
Overheads	£130,000	£10.00
Total	£299,000	£23.00

Task 1.12

Element	Unit cost
Materials	£1.00
Labour	£0.75
Overheads	£0.20
Total	£1.95

Section 2

Task 2.1

Manufacturing Account   Y/e 31 December

	£
Opening inventory of raw materials	27,500
Purchases of raw materials	135,000
Closing inventory of raw materials	35,000
DIRECT MATERIALS USED	127,500
Direct labour	252,500
PRIME COST	380,000
Manufacturing overheads	142,500
MANUFACTURING COST	522,500
Opening inventory of work in progress	30,000
Closing inventory of work in progress	35,000
COST OF GOODS MANUFACTURED	517,500
Opening inventory of finished goods	85,000
Closing inventory of finished goods	72,500
COST OF GOODS SOLD	530,000

Task 2.2

Characteristic	FIFO	LIFO	AVCO
The earliest invoice prices are used up first, working forward through to the latest prices	✓		
The most recent purchases are issued first		✓	
The best method if inventories are mixed when they are stored			✓

Task 2.3

	True	False
LIFO costs issues of inventory at the oldest purchase price		✓
AVCO costs issues of inventory at the oldest purchase price		✓
FIFO costs issues of inventory at the oldest purchase price	✓	
LIFO values closing inventory at the most recent purchase price		✓
FIFO values closing inventory at the most recent purchase price	✓	
AVCO values closing inventory at the latest purchase price		✓

Task 2.4

Method	Cost of issue on 18 August	Closing inventory at 31 August
FIFO	(1,500 + 4,000 + (1,000/1,250 × 7,500)) = **£11,500**	(250/1,250 × 7,500) + 6,000 = **£7,500**
LIFO	(7,500 + 4,000 + (50/300 × 1,500)) = **£11,750**	(6,000 +(250/300 × 1,500)) = **£7,250**
AVCO	(2,100/2,350 × 13,000) = **£11,617**	(6,000 + (250/2,350 × 13,000)) = **£7,383**

Task 2.5

	True	False
The fixed cost per unit rises over the level of output		✓
The variable cost per unit remains constant over the level of output	✓	

Task 2.6

Characteristic	Time-rate	Piecework	Time-rate with overtime
Payment is made for each unit or task successfully completed		✓	
Workers are paid a day rate based on the hours they work	✓		
Overtime is paid for hours in excess of the basic agreed level			✓

Task 2.7

Payment method	Time-rate	Piecework
Production problems won't lead to a cut in pay	✓	
Incentives to produce more		✓
Quality less of a priority with this method	✓	

Task 2.8

Worker	Hours worked	Basic wage	Overtime	Gross wage
S Toni	35 hours	£490	£0	£490
A Partridge	39 hours	£490	£112	£602

Task 2.9

Worker	Units produced in week	Gross wage
C Hynde	450	£292.50
D Harry	390	£253.50

Task 2.10

Worker	Hours worked	Units produced	Basic wage	Bonus	Gross wage
M Jagger	35	130	£402.50	£0	£402.50
K Richard	35	139	£402.50	£0	£402.50
C Watts	35	160	£402.50	£30	£432.50

Task 2.11

	True	False
Variances only measure the difference between budgeted and actual cost and not budgeted and actual income		✓
An unfavourable variance means budgeted costs are greater than actual costs		✓

Task 2.12

Cost type	Budget £	Actual £	Variance	Adverse/Favourable
Direct materials	14,500	12,200	£2,300	F
Direct labour	5,000	3,125	£1,875	F
Production overheads	4,000	6,120	£2,120	A
Administration overheads	3,000	4,950	£1,950	A
Selling and Distribution overheads	5,000	2,950	£2,050	F

Task 2.13

Cost type	Budget	Variance	Adverse/ Favourable	Significant/ Not significant
Direct materials	£5,000	£335	Adverse	NS
Direct labour	£7,000	£815	Adverse	S
Production overheads	£6,000	£428	Favourable	NS
Administration overheads	£4,000	£580	Adverse	S
Selling and Distribution overheads	£2,000	£150	Adverse	NS

Task 2.14

Variance	Relevant manager
Direct material cost	Production manager
Advertising and sales overheads	Sales manager

BPP PRACTICE ASSESSMENT 6
BASIC COSTING

Time allowed: 2 hours

Basic Costing BPP practice assessment 6

Section 1

Task 1.1

Read the descriptions below and match them to the type of system by putting a tick in the correct box.

Description	Management accounting	Financial accounting
Purchase invoices are entered into the purchases day book		
Invoices are analysed to determine whether they are materials or expenses		
The costs on the invoice are added to costs already collected for a cost centre		
Individual invoices are posted to creditor accounts		

Task 1.2

Hawes Ltd makes goats' cheese in its creamery.

Classify the following costs by element (materials, labour or overheads) by putting a tick in the relevant column of the table below.

Cost	Materials	Labour	Overheads
Milk from goats delivered to the creamery			
Electricity charges for offices			
Wages of workers employed to churn the cheese			
Salary of the supervisor on the workshop floor			

Task 1.3

Kilnsey Ltd is in business as a walking boot shop selling boots and making repairs.

Classify the following costs by nature (direct or indirect) by putting a tick in the relevant column of the table below.

Cost	Direct	Indirect
Wages of cobbler employed to repair the boots		
Rent and rates for shop and workshop		
Licences paid per item to boot suppliers to stock their boots		
Oil for stitching machine		

Task 1.4

Pateley Ltd makes fishing rods.

Classify the following costs by function (production, administration, or financing) by putting a tick in the relevant column of the table below.

Cost	Production	Administration	Financing
Nylon line used in the rods			
Wages of manager's secretary			
Loan interest paid yearly			
Salary of employee making the fishing rods			

Task 1.5

Blubberhouses Ltd smokes fish and beef for sale.

Classify the following costs by their behaviour (fixed, variable, or semi-variable) by putting a tick in the relevant column of the table below.

Cost	Fixed	Variable	Semi-variable
Smoking of salmon fillets			
Salary of supervisor on the workshop floor			
Gas costs for the smoking machines that include a standing charge			
Basic element of labour costs paid on a time-rate basis			

Task 1.6

Birstwith Ltd makes dog accessories. It uses an alpha-numerical coding structure based on one profit centre and three cost centres as outlined below. Each code has a sub-code so each transaction will be coded as */***.

Profit/Cost centre	Code	Sub-classification	Sub-code
Sales	A	UK sales	100
		Overseas sales	200
Production	B	Direct cost	100
		Indirect cost	200
Administration	C	Direct cost	100
		Indirect cost	200
Selling and Distribution	D	Direct cost	100
		Indirect cost	200

Code the following revenue and expense transactions, which have been extracted from purchase invoices, sales invoices and payroll, using the table below.

Transaction	Code
Telephone charges for the payroll department	
Factory business rates	
Sales to the USA	
Sales to London	
Material for dog blankets	
Salary of sales representative	

Task 1.7

Dales Limited operates a restaurant and uses a coding system for its elements of cost (materials, labour or overheads) and then further classifies each element by nature (direct or indirect cost) as below. So, for example, the code for direct materials is A100.

Element of cost	Code	Nature of cost	Code
Materials	A	Direct	100
		Indirect	200
Labour	B	Direct	100
		Indirect	200
Overheads	C	Direct	100
		Indirect	200

Code the following costs, extracted from invoices and payroll, using the table below.

Cost	Code
Solicitor fees for arranging restaurant licence	
Fresh vegetables bought in daily from local farmers	
Waiting staff salaries	
Cleaning materials used by restaurant cleaners	
Security manager salary	

Task 1.8

Identify the following statements as either True or False by putting a tick in the relevant column of the table below.

	True	False
Step fixed costs show a sudden jump in cost to a new level when expansion goes beyond a certain level		
With variable costs each unit of output causes the same amount of cost to be incurred		
Direct costs are generally fixed		

Task 1.9

Classify the following costs as either fixed or variable by putting a tick in the relevant column of the table below.

Costs	Fixed	Variable
Fees for bookkeeper to write up accounts		
Glue for repairing books		
Salary of supervisor in warehouse		
Cake mix for wedding cake production line in bakery		

Task 1.10

Complete the table below showing fixed costs, variable costs, total costs and unit cost at the different levels of production

Units	Fixed costs	Variable costs	Total costs	Unit cost
1,000	£8,800	£3,500	£12,300	£12.30
2,000				
3,000				
4,000				

Task 1.11

Burnsall Ltd is costing a single product, which has the following cost details:

Variable costs per unit

Materials	£10.50
Labour	£12.45
Total fixed costs	£13,000

Complete the following total cost and unit cost table for a production level of 13,000 units.

Element	Total cost	Unit cost
Materials		
Labour		
Overheads		
Total		

Task 1.12

Skipton Ltd makes a single product and for a production level of 12,000 units has the following cost details:

Materials 3,000 kilos at	£10 per kilo
Labour 4,000 hours at	£15 an hour
Overheads	£30,000

Complete the table below to show the unit cost at the production level of 12,000 units.

Element	Unit cost
Materials	
Labour	
Overheads	
Total	

Section 2

Task 2.1

Reorder the following headings and costs into a manufacturing account format on the right side of the table below for the year ended 31 December.

Heading	Cost £'000	Manufacturing account	£'000
Closing inventory of work in progress	8,300		
Direct labour	12,800		
Opening inventory of raw materials	7,500		
Closing inventory of finished goods	45,700		
Closing inventory of raw materials	5,600		
Manufacturing overheads	10,250		
COST OF GOODS SOLD	38,400		
MANUFACTURING COST	37,950		
Purchases of raw materials	13,000		
Opening inventory of work in progress	9,850		
Opening inventory of finished goods	44,600		
PRIME COST	27,700		
DIRECT MATERIALS USED	14,900		
COST OF GOODS MANUFACTURED	39,500		

Task 2.2

Identify the correct inventory valuation method from the characteristic given by putting a tick in the relevant column of the table below.

Characteristic	FIFO	LIFO	AVCO
Gives the largest inventory valuation if purchase prices are rising			
Gives the lowest value of closing inventory if prices are rising			
Issues and closing inventory are based on average purchase prices			

Task 2.3

Identify whether the following statements are True or False by putting a tick in the relevant column of the table below.

	True	False
Finished goods are ready for sale		
Raw materials is inventory which is partially completed		
Work in progress is partially completed		

Task 2.4

Ripon Ltd has the following movements in a certain type of inventory into and out of its stores for the month of October:

DATE	RECEIPTS		ISSUES	
	Units	Cost	Units	Cost
October 5	300	£900		
October 8	600	£2,400		
October 12	500	£2,500		
October 18			1,200	
October 25	1,000	£6,000		

Complete the table below for the issue and closing inventory values.

Method	Cost of issue on 18 October	Closing inventory at 31 October
FIFO		
LIFO		
AVCO		

Task 2.5

Identify the following statements as True or False by putting a tick in the relevant column of the table below.

	True	False
The fixed cost per unit rises over the level of output		
The variable cost per unit falls over the level of output		

Task 2.6

For each of the following characteristics, identify the labour payment method by putting a tick in the relevant column of the table below.

Characteristic	Time-rate	Piecework	Piecework plus bonus
Workers paid under this method are encouraged to produce more at all levels of activity			
A basic amount is paid per hour worked			
A bonus is paid for output in excess of that expected			

Task 2.7

Identify one advantage for each labour payment method by putting a tick in the relevant column of the table below.

Advantage	Time-rate	Piecework
If production fluctuates, pay will still be the same		
This method encourages higher production		
Fewer inspectors may be needed with this method		

Task 2.8

Settle Ltd pays a time-rate of £10 per hour to its direct labour for a standard 37.5-hour week. Any of the labour force working in excess of 37.5 hours is paid an overtime rate of £12 per hour.

Calculate the gross wage for the week for the two workers in the table below.

Worker	Hours worked	Basic wage	Overtime	Gross wage
N Crane	37.5			
F Crane	39			

Task 2.9

Leyburn Ltd uses a piecework method to pay labour in one of its factories. The rate used is 95p per unit produced.

Calculate the gross wage for the week for the two workers in the table below.

Worker	Units produced in week	Gross wage
P Freire	925	
J Rousseau	870	

Task 2.10

Richmond Ltd uses a time-rate method with bonus to pay its direct labour in one of its factories. The time-rate used is £9.75 per hour and a worker is expected to produce five units an hour, anything over this and the worker is paid a bonus of £1.50 per unit.

Calculate the gross wage for the week including bonus for the three workers in the table below.

Worker	Hours worked	Units produced	Basic wage	Bonus	Gross wage
U Bolt	35	175			
C Ohuruogu	35	205			
S Coe	35	210			

Task 2.11

Identify the following statements as being True or False by putting a tick in the relevant column of the table below.

	True	False
Variances measure the difference between budgeted and actual cost and income		
A favourable variance means budgeted costs are greater than actual costs		

Task 2.12

Masham Ltd has produced a performance report detailing budgeted and actual cost for last month.

Calculate the amount of the variance for each cost type and then determine whether it is adverse or favourable by typing F for favourable and A for adverse in the right-hand column of the table below.

Cost type	Budget £	Actual £	Variance	Adverse/ Favourable
Direct materials	4,250	5,200		
Direct labour	5,100	3,125		
Production overheads	3,750	6,125		
Administration overheads	3,250	4,975		
Selling and Distribution overheads	1,900	2,850		

Task 2.13

The following performance report for this month has been produced for Catterick Ltd as summarised in the table below. Any variance in excess of 10% of budget is deemed to be significant and should be reported to the relevant manager for review and appropriate action.

Examine the variances in the table below and indicate whether they are significant or not significant by typing S for significant and NS for not significant in the right-hand column below.

Cost type	Budget £	Variance	Adverse/ Favourable	Significant/ Not significant
Direct materials	£45,000	£335	Adverse	
Direct labour	£27,000	£815	Adverse	
Production overheads	£16,000	£2,428	Favourable	
Administration overheads	£14,000	£580	Adverse	
Selling and Distribution overheads	£12,000	£1,500	Adverse	

Task 2.14

It was noted from the performance report for Three Bridges Ltd for an earlier month that the following cost variances were significant:

- Direct material cost
- Administration overheads

These variances need to be reported to the relevant managers for review and appropriate action, if required.

Identify a relevant manager for each significant variance to whom the performance report should be sent.

Variance	Relevant manager
Direct material cost	▼
Administration overheads	▼

Picklist:

Production manager
Sales manager
HR manager
Administration manager

BPP PRACTICE ASSESSMENT 6
BASIC COSTING

ANSWERS

Basic Costing BPP practice assessment 6

Section 1

Task 1.1

Description	Management accounting	Financial accounting
Purchase invoices are entered into the purchases day book		✓
Invoices are analysed to determine whether they are materials or expenses	✓	
The costs on the invoice are added to costs already collected for a cost centre	✓	
Individual invoices are posted to creditor accounts		✓

Task 1.2

Cost	Materials	Labour	Overheads
Milk from goats delivered to the creamery	✓		
Electricity charges for offices			✓
Wages of workers employed to churn the cheese		✓	
Salary of the supervisor on the workshop floor			✓

Task 1.3

Cost	Direct	Indirect
Wages of cobbler employed to repair the boots	✓	
Rent and rates for shop and workshop		✓
Licences paid per item to boot suppliers to stock their boots	✓	
Oil for stitching machine		✓

Task 1.4

Cost	Production	Administration	Financing
Nylon line used in the rods	✓		
Wages of manager's secretary		✓	
Loan interest paid yearly			✓
Salary of employee making the fishing rods	✓		

Task 1.5

Cost	Fixed	Variable	Semi-variable
Smoking of salmon fillets		✓	
Salary of supervisor on the workshop floor	✓		
Gas costs for the smoking machines that include a standing charge			✓
Basic element of labour costs paid on a time-rate basis	✓		

Task 1.6

Transaction	Code
Telephone charges for the payroll department	C/200
Factory business rates	B/200
Sales to the USA	A/200
Sales to London	A/100
Material for dog blankets	B/100
Salary of sales representative	D/100

Task 1.7

Cost	Code
Solicitor fees for arranging restaurant licence	C200
Fresh vegetables bought in daily from local farmers	A100
Waiting staff salaries	B100
Cleaning materials used by restaurant cleaners	A200
Security manager salary	B200

Task 1.8

	True	False
Step fixed costs show a sudden jump in cost to a new level when expansion goes beyond a certain level	✓	
With variable costs each unit of output causes the same amount of cost to be incurred	✓	
Direct costs are generally fixed		✓

Task 1.9

Costs	Fixed	Variable
Fees for bookkeeper to write-up accounts	✓	
Glue for repairing books		✓
Salary of supervisor in warehouse	✓	
Cake mix for wedding cake production line in bakery		✓

Task 1.10

Units	Fixed costs	Variable costs	Total costs	Unit cost
1,000	£8,800	£3,500	£12,300	£12.30
2,000	£8,800	£7,000	£15,800	£7.90
3,000	£8,800	£10,500	£19,300	£6.43
4,000	£8,800	£14,000	£22,800	£5.70

Task 1.11

Element	Total cost	Unit cost
Materials	£136,500	£10.50
Labour	£161,850	£12.45
Overheads	£13,000	£1.00
Total	£311,350	£23.95

Task 1.12

Element	Unit cost
Materials	£2.50
Labour	£5.00
Overheads	£2.50
Total	£10.00

Section 2

Task 2.1

Manufacturing Account   Y/e 31 December

Heading	Cost £'000		£'000
Closing inventory of work in progress	8,300	Opening inventory of raw materials	7,500
Direct labour	12,800	Purchases of raw materials	13,000
Opening inventory of raw materials	7,500	Closing inventory of raw materials	5,600
Closing inventory of finished goods	45,700	DIRECT MATERIALS USED	14,900
Closing inventory of raw materials	5,600	Direct labour	12,800
Manufacturing overheads	10,250	PRIME COST	27,700
COST OF GOODS SOLD	38,400	Manufacturing Overheads	10,250
MANUFACTURING COST	37,950	MANUFACTURING COST	37,950
Purchases of raw materials	13,000	Opening inventory of work in progress	9,850
Opening inventory of work in progress	9,850	Closing inventory of work in progress	8,300
Opening inventory of finished goods	44,600	COST OF GOODS MANUFACTURED	39,500
PRIME COST	27,700	Opening inventory of finished goods	44,600
DIRECT MATERIALS USED	14,900	Closing inventory of finished goods	45,700
COST OF GOODS MANUFACTURED	39,500	COST OF GOODS SOLD	38,400

Task 2.2

Characteristic	FIFO	LIFO	AVCO
Gives the largest inventory valuation if purchase prices are rising	✓		
Gives the lowest value of closing inventory if prices are rising		✓	
Issues and closing inventory are based on average purchase prices			✓

Task 2.3

	True	False
Finished goods are ready for sale	✓	
Raw materials is inventory which is partially completed		✓
Work in progress is partially completed	✓	

Task 2.4

Method	Cost of issue on 18 October	Closing inventory at 31 October
FIFO	(900 + 2,400 + (300/500 × 2,500)) = **£4,800**	(6,000 + (200/500 × 2,500)) = **£7,000**
LIFO	(2,500 + 2,400 + (100/300 × 900)) = **£5,200**	(6,000 + (200/300 × 900)) = **£6,600**
AVCO	(1,200/1,400 × 5,800) = **£4,971**	(6,000 + (200/1,400 × 5,800)) = **£6,829**

Task 2.5

	True	False
The fixed cost per unit rises over the level of output		✓
The variable cost per unit falls over the level of output		✓

Task 2.6

Payment method	Time-rate	Piecework	Piecework plus bonus
Workers paid under this method are encouraged to produce more at all levels of activity		✓	
A basic amount is paid per hour worked	✓		
A bonus is paid for output in excess of that expected			✓

Task 2.7

Advantage	Time-rate	Piecework
If production fluctuates, pay will still be the same	✓	
This method encourages higher production		✓
Fewer inspectors may be needed with this method	✓	

Task 2.8

Worker	Hours worked	Basic wage	Overtime	Gross wage
N Crane	37.5	£375.00	£0.00	£375.00
F Crane	39	£375.00	£18.00	£393.00

Task 2.9

Worker	Units produced in week	Gross wage
P Freire	925	£878.75
J Rousseau	870	£826.50

Task 2.10

Worker	Hours worked	Units produced	Basic wage	Bonus	Gross wage
U Bolt	35	175	£341.25	£0.00	£341.25
S Ohuruogu	35	205	£341.25	£45.00	£386.25
S Coe	35	210	£341.25	£52.50	£393.75

Task 2.11

	True	False
Variances measure the difference between budgeted and actual cost and income	✓	
A favourable variance means budgeted costs are greater than actual costs	✓	

Task 2.12

Cost type	Budget £	Actual £	Variance	Adverse/Favourable
Direct materials	4,250	5,200	£950	A
Direct labour	5,100	3,125	£1,975	F
Production overheads	3,750	6,125	£2,375	A
Administration overheads	3,250	4,975	£1,725	A
Selling and Distribution overheads	1,900	2,850	£950	A

Task 2.13

Cost type	Budget £	Variance	Adverse/ Favourable	Significant/ Not significant
Direct materials	£45,000	£335	Adverse	NS
Direct labour	£27,000	£815	Adverse	NS
Production overheads	£16,000	£2,428	Favourable	S
Administration overheads	£14,000	£580	Adverse	NS
Selling and Distribution overheads	£12,000	£1,500	Adverse	S

Task 2.14

Variance	Relevant manager
Direct material cost	Production manager
Administration overheads	Administration manager

Notes

Notes

Notes

Notes

Notes

Notes

Notes